Also by Charlamagne Tha God

Black Privilege

Shook One

Get Honest or Die Lying

Why Small Talk Sucks

Charlamagne Tha God

BLACK PRIVILEGE
PUBLISHING

ATRIA

New York London Toronto Sydney New Delhi

BLACK
PRIVILEGE
PUBLISHING

ATRIA

An Imprint of Simon & Schuster, LLC
1230 Avenue of the Americas
New York, NY 10020

First Black Privilege Publishing/Atria Books hardcover edition May 2024

BLACK PRIVILEGE PUBLISHING **/ ATRIA** BOOKS and colophon are
trademarks of Simon & Schuster, LLC

Simon & Schuster: Celebrating 100 Years of Publishing in 2024

For information about special discounts for bulk purchases, please contact Simon &
Schuster Special Sales at 1-866-506-1949 or business@simonandschuster.com.

The Simon & Schuster Speakers Bureau can bring authors to your live event.
For more information or to book an event, contact the Simon & Schuster Speakers
Bureau at 1-866-248-3049 or visit our website at www.simonspeakers.com.

Interior design by Silverglass

Manufactured in the United States of America

1 3 5 7 9 10 8 6 4 2

Library of Congress Control Number: 2024933965

ISBN 978-1-9821-7379-1

ISBN 978-1-9821-7381-4 (ebook)

This book is dedicated to all the earthlings, extraterrestrials, and spiritual beings living a human existence who don't engage in small talk. You are my tribe.

Contents

Introduction:
No More Small Talk

My name is Lenard Larry McKelvey, and I absolutely *hate* small talk.

I hate it the way kids hate when their tablet time is over. ("Hey, that's enough *Roblox*.")

I hate it the way that Black people hate white supremacy.

I hate it the way white supremacists hate Black people.

Now, if you know me by my alter ego, Charlamagne Tha God, then you might be shocked to learn I could hate anything that involves talking.

Be it on the radio, TV, or podcasts, I've done a lot of talking over the last few decades. And trust me, I was running my mouth long before I ever got in front of a microphone. Just like I'll still be running my mouth whenever I decide to put down the mic for the last time.

But for the thousands of hours I've been talking to audiences over those years, what you haven't heard me participate in is too much *small talk*.

Don't get it twisted, there have been plenty of jokes, conversations with my cohosts, "Donkeys of the Day," some moments where I let myself get worked up on-air about something for effect (I'm an entertainer after all), and long, insightful, and sometimes even uncomfortable talks with the guests I've been so lucky to have visit my platforms.

But SMALL TALK? Nah.

— — —

In 2018 I had a three-hour-long conversation with a chocolate-covered white supremacist named Kanye West as we walked around his ranch in Wyoming. I left realizing that Kanye is VERY intentional about everything he does. That's why I've never felt sorry for him when he self-sabotages. Yes, Kanye has been blessed with power and money, but even the most brilliant amongst us can submit our will to the white devil in us. And Kanye makes that choice quite often.

On the other end of the spectrum, I've had incredible sit-downs with my childhood hero, the author Judy Blume. I, a young Black kid in the Deep South, always loved the white, best-selling children's book author because Judy showed me a world I'd never have known or seen otherwise. She wrote to give voice to young people and treat them with respect, especially young girls, which I appreciate even more today as a father to my own daughters. Judy is also very intentional about everything she does, but the difference between her and a Kanye is that Judy's intentions are not self-serving. You will never lose if you understand that your true purpose in life is service to others, and that's what Judy chooses to do with her art.

And not to compare myself to Judy (trust when I say she's on her own level, above mine or anyone else's honestly), but I try to bring that same mentality to my work too. I've talked to rappers, presidential candidates, moguls, activists, ballers, therapists, criminals, comedians, authors, preachers, hell, even cartoon characters! (Uncle Ruckus, no relation.) You'll hear me crack up and push people and talk shit sometimes, but what you won't hear in all those hours' worth of content is much *small talk*. (I purposely talk to artists before we start taping specifically so I can get any mindless chitchat out of the way.)

That's because when it comes to conversation, one thing I'm not going to do is beat around the bush.

Or schmooze.

Or spend time talking about small shit.

That's never been my style. If I'm sitting down with someone for a conversation, I'm going to get straight to the point.

I can't lie, there have been times where I've been a little too straightforward. Where I could have stood to schmooze a bit before I got down to business.

But for better or worse, that's not how I'm wired.

For as long as I can remember, I've been direct. Maybe it's a result of being the son of a father who was often painfully direct himself, who would always tell me the fastest way between two points is a straight line. (You'll read more about my Pops later.) Maybe it's because for much of my life I was so anxious in social settings that I just wanted to get things over with, rather than prolong the uneasiness.

Wherever the impulse came from, my directness has served me very well in life. It helped *The Breakfast Club* become one of the most popular shows in the world (it even landed me in the Radio Hall of Fame). It helped me become the host of several TV shows and launch a popular podcast, *The Brilliant Idiots*, which has been running for ten years. It even helped me become a *New York Times* best-selling author.

All that time, my aversion to small talk has been my superpower. My *extra*.

Now I want to encourage you to make rejecting small talk a priority in your own life. Not just for you, but for me too. And for my kids.

Because small talk is killing us as a society.

To be clear, when I say "small talk" here I'm not just saying you can't chat about the weather or ask coworkers how traffic was on the way to the job.

I mean *small talk* as a symbol of our lack of authentic communication. Both as individuals and collectively.

I realize that might sound a little wild, like a nut-ass thing to say.

At first glance, it seems like communication is at an all-time high.

We talk on the phone. We text. We DM. We go live. We post videos. We make clips. We TikTok. We send VMs.

Sometimes, it seems like all we do now is talk with each other.

But if you look closer at all that communicating, you'll find that most of the time we're talking *at* each other, instead of *with* one another and we rarely discuss anything that truly matters.

Social media should be elevating our conversations. Instead, it's dragging us down to the lowest common denominator.

We have more access to each other than at any time in human history, but somehow we're still stuck on *small talk*. We avoid the big questions by filling our minds with fluff. Nonsense intended to distract and delay action and learning, rather than encourage growth and understanding.

Small talk about God.

Small talk about race.

Small talk about our fears.

Small talk about our kids.

Small talk about our dreams.

Small talk about our mental health.

Remember, when it comes to talk, quantity does not equal quality.

If anything, the opposite is true. (I write this as a professional talker, but I promise this will all make sense.)

In this book, I'm going to encourage you to *say* less, but *do* more.

Is that hypocritical advice from me of all people?

Maybe.

But I have no choice. I don't know about you, but I can't take the noise anymore.

Have there been moments where important and impactful conversations rose above the noise?

Yes, I believe that happened with the conversation around George Floyd and Black Lives Matter. Just as it happened with the conversation around the #MeToo Movement.

Those moments showed us what was possible. But where have those conversations gone?

It's not like there's a shortage of important things to converse about. And yet somehow, we manage to keep avoiding them.

Instead we reward *small talkers* for being performative with their conversations. You know the type. At first glance, they seem committed to addressing serious issues. Racism. The environment. Mental health. But scratch even just a little bit below the surface and it becomes obvious that they're not talking because they want to fix things, but because it gets them engagement:

Likes.

Clicks.

Views.

They don't have a committed POV, they're just committed to creating content.

But where's the *intent*?

Well, in this book I'm going to have those major conversations. I'm going to address a lot of the dialogue that people are trying to talk around, under, and over.

Anything but head-on.

We're going to have those hard *big talks* in this book because the alternative is a lot more difficult than any conversation could ever be.

— — —

Have you ever heard the saying "Un-Big Your Back"?

It's basically social media's way of telling someone they need to lose weight.

(Which surprised me, because usually when people focus on you being obese, the first thing they talk about is your stomach. Like how the internet was calling Lizzo "R. Belly" in response to allegations she had mistreated employees and backup dancers, or when folks started calling Beanie Sigel "Butt and Gut" after he gained some weight.)

Leave it to the creative hive of social media to pinpoint how someone's back can grow too big when they put on some pounds. Hence, "Un-Big Your Back."

I'm going to take that phrase and rework it for this book. One of my goals here is to help you "Un-Small Your Brain."

That's because our outlooks on life tend to get smaller and smaller as we get older. And ironically, I notice this with people who have had the "privilege" of higher education. Often when a person has an area of expertise, they tend to stay in the comfort zone that expertise has given them. Anything that disturbs the peace, they block. They don't want to be challenged because they've literally been told they know it all.

Once someone has a diploma with their name on it above someone else's (photocopied) signature, they lose sight of how much more education they could obtain by remaining open to new ideas and conversations. By accepting that degrees are checkpoints, not finish lines.

I never went to college, which used to make me anxious in certain settings. I figured I was missing out on a secret. Some kind of intelligence that people with college degrees had picked up. But the older I get, the more I realize that my lack of higher education, and my approach to spaces where that made me the outlier, has worked in my favor.

By being aware that I *don't* know it all, I'm forced to ask questions. I'm forced to seek out new information and perspectives. I'm forced to think big, instead of laying back in my comfort zone.

Which is why I want all of you to think big too.

While we're talking about my lack of a college degree, I want to share a little bit about my background for those who've never listened to anything I do, including, but not limited to, listening to *The Breakfast Club* or the *Brilliant Idiots* podcast, or reading my first book, *Black Privilege*.

I grew up in a single-wide trailer on a dirt road in Moncks Corner, South Carolina (population when I was growing up was in the seven thousands).

My mother was a Jehovah's Witness public school teacher who never made over $30,000 a year. My aforementioned father was an unrepentant hustler. He was a strong presence in my life, but he also struggled with drugs and alcohol. He talked a good game about responsibility, but the example he set for me was dysfunctional at best.

I didn't have anything handed to me.

I grew up with cornfields as my playground. I graduated from night school because I got kicked out of two high schools. I spent more time in jail as a young man (forty-five days) than I did in college (you already know). Most of my cousins and childhood friends wound up, as my father would put it, "either in jail, dead, or drunk under a tree."

Yet in just over twenty-five years, I've managed to build one of the biggest platforms in media.

And one of the reasons I was able to keep moving up the entertainment ladder was because I've been able to *evolve*.

I refused to stay stuck in one place.

It was a minor miracle that I talked my way into becoming a personality on radio station Z93 Jamz in Charleston, South Carolina.

But I wanted more. Just like I exceeded any reasonable hopes for myself when I got on the air doing mornings in Philadelphia. But I was still looking for more.

Landing in NYC and building *The Breakfast Club*, the biggest syndicated hip-hop show in the nation, should have been the culmination of my dreams, but nope. I've branched out into books and TV. And still have a lot more I want to accomplish.

Every step of the journey, I tried to soak up as much information and wisdom as I could, and then apply it to my life.

I refused to get comfortable in whatever little step I'd made and stayed focused on evolving into the best version of myself I could possibly be.

Which is what I need us to collectively start doing as a society.

But not for me. I have four incredible daughters. Beautiful Black girls who are my greatest blessings. I feel tremendous responsibility for them. Not only for them at home, but also in the world at large.

I need them to walk into a world that is focused on the important issues.

Not the small talk that passes for meaningful conversation these days.

— — —

You'll notice the title of this book is *Get Honest or Die Lying*.

Why did I choose that?

The first reason, of course, is to pay respect to 50 Cent's classic debut album, *Get Rich or Die Tryin'*. Anytime I can work a hip-hop reference into this book, I'm going to do it. If you were born in the 1900s like I was, then I'm assuming you all are going to know all my references, but if for some reason you don't, ask one of your uncles. You know, the type who hates all this "mumble rap," wears construction Timberlands and denim shorts in the summer? Yeah, those are the best hip-hop heads, so any references from the 1900s hip-hop culture I make, ask him to translate.

Most of the hip-hop references are going to be celebratory. But I'm also a firm believer that if you want the people around you to have hard conversations, you must lead the way by starting with the conversations that are hard for you.

So in this book, I'm going to have a difficult conversation about hip-hop. There's no doubt that the culture has had a positive impact on me and my community. It's given us so much great music and beautiful moments. It's given a voice to people who were voiceless. And yes, it's made a lot of us serious money. It's allowed us to better our lives and the lives of our family and friends.

But the BIGGER conversation is "At what cost?"

I came up during the nineties and early 2000s, when a lot of rappers realized that talking about gangsta topics (things they would never actually do themselves) was a path to making millions of dollars. To me, when you're promoting violent content strictly for the sake of profit, that's a very dangerous form of small talk.

That moment is where things got ugly. Soon you had whole generations of youngsters saying, "Well, these guys have been providing the soundtrack to our lives, but we really live it! So if we really live it, we might as well rap about it too!" The micro-minded voices in hip-hop were getting macro exposure, and it led to way too much small-minded content in rap.

When I think of how the elders that came before us, folks like KRS-One and Chuck D, understood the power of hip-hop, but we misused it, I'll be honest—it kind of saddens me. If more artists would have listened to those elders, then a whole generation of people—including my generation—would have been influenced to speak to larger issues impacting our community, instead of wasting so much time on the small shit.

You currently have a whole generation of individuals, myself included, doing countless hours of therapy in order to heal from trauma that we should have addressed thirty years ago. My good brother Resmaa Menakem said in his book *My Grandmother's Hands*, "Change culture and you change lives. You can also change the course of history."

And given the cultural power hip-hop has harnessed over the past fifty years, maybe we could have elevated the conversation *globally*.

I want this book to be a small step in re-harnessing, and re-focusing, that power and using it to get those conversations started.

— — —

Before we get all the way into some serious conversations, I need to stress that this book is going to be a little different than my first two.

The first difference is that the chapters are going to be shorter in this one. I realized that books hold my attention more when I feel like I'm tearing through chapters. Not to mention these days the majority of people are conditioned to reading captions and comments on social media and YouTube. I want this book to be just as digestible. Sometimes Mohammad must go to the mountain.

The focus is going to be different too. *Black Privilege* was about my story, following that path that took me from the dirt road I grew up on to the top of the media game and the life lessons I learned along the way.

My second book, *Shook One*, was me opening up about the anxiety and bouts of depression I've been dealing with my whole life and the methods I've learned to deal with them, in particular what I was realizing about myself in therapy.

This book will still share parts of my personal journey (a lot has definitely happened over the last few years) and my ongoing battles with anxiety (I'm literally wearing a heart monitor right now because I keep convincing myself I'm about to have a heart attack), but those won't be the focus this time.

No, my first two books were mainly about my personal journey. Now I'm turning the lens around and taking a hard look at *y'all*. In the first two books I was talking about myself. Now I'm going to talk about all of US.

We've already touched on some of the topics we're going to have some major-league conversations about, like social media, hip-hop, and mental health. But there are a lot of other hard convos we're going to have inside these pages too.

Probably at the top of the list is politics. We're going to talk about the Democrats and the Republicans. And we're going to name names: folks like a woman I once had high (insert your own "she smoked weed in college to Tupac" joke here) hopes for, Kamala Harris, and another I've never had any hope for, Marjorie Taylor Greene; and of course Joe Biden and Donald Trump.

We're also going to talk about entitlement. Don't get me wrong; I often felt I deserved more growing up, but I was willing to put in the work to get it. These kids today really believe that they should receive the fruits of one's labor without having to do one's labor.

We're going to discuss people who think they know everything, like those college graduates I just mentioned. I used to hear people say, "I don't know nuthin!" when asked about the world, and I thought that was an ignorant mindset. But I've learned it's actually one of the most freeing feelings in the world!! When you don't try to front but freely admit you're not up to speed on something, *that's* when you begin to learn.

We're going to talk about patience. Or the lack thereof. This generation is always in a rush to go nowhere. And when I say "generation," I'm not referring to anyone's age. I'm referring to this generation of humans who are plugged into the same matrix. We worship the high-light reels, but ignore the work that went into making those high-lights possible in the first place.

We're going to address one of the big lies that this country was built on, which is that free speech is actually free. While it is true that you can say whatever you want, that doesn't mean you are free from the consequences of said free speech; there is absolutely a price to pay for every word that comes out of your mouth.

And we're absolutely going to get candid about "cancel culture." I've evolved a lot, I like to think for the better, over the years. But my greatest changes have come from wanting to do better for myself and my family, not from being "shamed" into a change by outside voices.

We're going to ask, Whatever happened to manners? My grandmother always would tell me manners will take you where money won't, but I guess everyone is getting too much money because they clearly move like they don't need manners. There are no boundaries anymore. People will just walk up to you and put a phone in your face, because all they care about is the attention they will get on their social media, not once do they think they are violating your space.

We're going to talk about provincialism. That is a word I can barely pronounce and would never get the opportunity to use if I wasn't an author. I could have just said I'm sick of people who think the entire world revolves around America, but I would rather order a turkey and provincialism sandwich. . . .

As you can see, there's a lot of *big* talk to have.

And at the very least, I know this book is going to make me feel better because venting is therapeutic! And if I feel better, the world will be better because I am the man in the mirror that Michael Jackson was talking about.

Finally, you'll notice that I end each chapter with the words "Let's discuss." Now, if you follow me on social media or listen to me on

The Breakfast Club, then you already know I like to finish streams of consciousness using that phrase. I do that because I want everything I say (or write) to be opening the floor to a larger discussion. I'm not one of those people who believes they are an expert at anything, I just have experiences and my lived experience is what I rely on a majority of the time. So when I say, "Let's discuss," that's exactly what I want you to do when you put this book down. Have real, meaningful discussions with your family, friends, coworkers—whoever. In fact, when someone attempts to make #SmallTalk with you, I want you to say to them, "Charlamagne says we don't have to do this anymore. We can get real." Just put it all on me! I literally want you to reference this book when attempting to make conversation with folks! Because, man, the stakes are too high for us to stay silent!

CHAPTER 1

Small Talk to You Nice

Let's start with you.

I firmly believe that before you can have truly transformative conversations with other folks, you have to start by having hard, unflinching conversations with a very special person first:

Yourself.

I don't mean talking to yourself in the mirror like Robert De Niro in *Raging Bull* or muttering to yourself while you walk down the street.

Instead, I'm referring to a series of thoughtful conversations where you really commit to unlearning a lot of the bullshit and nonsense that got put into your head as a child. Conversations where you can begin to finally peel back the trauma, hurt, and insecurity that's been weighing you down and holding you back.

The type of conversations that come from going to therapy.

I know, I know. Therapy is not technically an act of talking to yourself. It involves sitting down with a trained professional (I'm going to introduce you to a great one later in this book) and letting that person guide you through a series of questions. Ones that are designed to help you understand what you're feeling in your life. How you've gotten here. And how you can get somewhere better.

And most importantly, questions that are asked without judgment. No trained therapist is going to roll their eyes or shake their head when you tell them something. No matter how crazy or weird it might sound.

Instead, they're going to help you contextualize the things that have happened to you in the past that have led you to making bad choices. That might have led you to feeling insecure about your condition. That might make you feel like you're starting to lose it.

This is very important for African-Americans to understand, because if you're Black, it's almost assured that you've suffered some sort of trauma in your life. Hopefully nothing as intense as what our ancestors experienced, but moments that still had a real impact on your life. They could range from microaggressions to straight-out racism to actual violence. But no matter where they ranged on that scale, I promise they impacted you in a real way. And I also bet your harmful experience wasn't an isolated incident. You've probably been dealing with these sorts of issues your entire life.

What makes getting past them even more challenging is that there's a real stigma against therapy and discussions about mental health in the African-American community. And the folks who undoubtedly need it the most are also the most skeptical about it. I broke down some of the reasons behind this in my last book, *Shook One: Anxiety Playing Tricks on Me*, so I won't repeat it all here.

But I will say that it's a stigma that hasn't completely disappeared. Even today, I'm dealing with other Black folks questioning my commitment to the cause of mental health. I've been called a "fake mental health advocate," or critics will say that I use discussions of mental health as a shield to distract folks from all the wild shit I used to talk about on the radio way back when.

So for the record: I started to work on my mental health because I knew that if I didn't deal with my trauma, my trauma would ultimately deal with me!

Because I'd been raised in an environment where mental health wasn't ever discussed, I didn't even have the vocabulary to articulate what I was feeling, especially in my early '30s when it felt like my career had stalled out. When you combine unhealed trauma, anxiety, depression, being broke at thirty-two, living at home with your mother and having a child to look after, that's a recipe for a lot of people to kill themselves. (Trust me, I thought about it every day.)

I was in a bad place.

An event that helped me put some of my struggles into focus came one day when I was driving down Interstate 26 in South Carolina. Suddenly my heart started pounding. Like it was about to jump out of my chest.

Remember how Redd Foxx used to grab his chest and say, "This is the big one!" in *Sanford and Son*? I literally did the same. You couldn't tell me I wasn't going to die out there on that road.

Most people would have at least pulled over, but I've never been accused of being "most folks." Instead, I kept on driving to where I'd been headed, a comedy show my guy Lil Duval was performing in Orangeburg, South Carolina. I'd had that feeling before, so I figured I'd make it through the night. And I did.

The next morning I took myself to the ER. When I explained my symptoms, they started performing tests immediately. EKGs. A chest X-ray. A blood test for troponin, a protein that signals you're having a heart attack. I had wires and tubes sticking out of me for hours.

Finally, a doctor came into the room to deliver his verdict.

"Well, you're not having a heart attack," he told me. "In fact, your heart is in tremendous shape. It's what we call an 'athlete's heart.'"

My breathing started to slow down a bit. "OK," I told myself, "I'm not going to die. Cool." But something was clearly wrong because I'd been having these types of attacks my whole life.

"Let me ask you a question," the doctor continued. "Do you suffer from anxiety?"

"Anxiety, what do you mean?" I asked him.

I honestly didn't *really know what that even meant* back then. I was thirty-something years old and couldn't tell you what anxiety looked like, felt like, or how it was supposed to be handled if you ever did get a diagnosis. I'd *heard* the word, of course, but that didn't mean I *knew* the word. At least nobody I'd ever been around talked about managing their anxiety.

"Well, based on your symptoms and your test results, it sounds like you suffered a panic attack while you were driving. Do you happen to be experiencing any stress at the moment?"

Was I experiencing any stress? Hell yeah I was experiencing stress.

My entire existence felt like one big ball of stress.

They discharged me with instructions to try to be more "mindful" and try working out and sleeping more.

I heard them, but I wasn't really *listening.*

To me, there was only one thing that was going to make me feel better and that was getting out of my momma's house and getting back on the air in a major market. I just needed to be in a better position. Once I had that, everything would be all right.

So that's what I set out to do. I worked my ass off networking, pitching, and politickin' till finally I got another shot, this time on the show that changed my life, *The Breakfast Club* in New York City.

And yes, it was a stressful environment to work in, but I wasn't worried. I was in the Big Apple. I was being heard every day by hundreds of thousands of people. I was inching closer and closer to my dream.

Eventually my wife and daughter were able to join me. Everything was starting to look up.

What I wasn't doing, however, was following that emergency room doctor's advice. I was getting less and less sleep and becoming less and less peaceful in my existence.

Instead, I was out in the streets most nights, drinking and smoking weed. Being a toxic crusader. My wife stuck by my side, but she knew I was full of shit. She couldn't stand how I was living. She knew I was going to eventually crash and burn and that was breaking her heart.

But on the surface, I was great. My star was rising, and I was getting everything I ever wanted out of this radio business.

And for the first time in my life I was making real money. Suddenly I had a nice house in New Jersey. I could have had a nice car, but I'm cheap, so I didn't go chasing Phantoms and Bentleys. I stuck to the same Cadillac Escalade with 200k miles on it that I was used to.

The days of waiting in line for unemployment checks and being thirty-two living in my childhood bedroom were in the rearview mirror. There was no question if this was a movie it would be my "look Momma I made it" moment.

But despite all the money, the celebrity interviews, the headlines, and the party lifestyle, I wasn't *happy*.

I'd still have moments where my heart would race and my breath would get short. Where it felt like the world was closing in on me and my sight would go dark. Where it felt like I was dying.

I tried seeing doctors again, but they kept telling me the same things:

"You're in the prime of your life."

"You have an athlete's heart."

"You're fine."

Sure, the one doctor had mentioned "anxiety," but that wasn't a real thing. Anxiety was something you felt for a second in a scary movie, or if your team was lining up for the game-winning field goal with a kicker who had just missed an extra point. It wasn't something that stayed with you.

So, what was it then?

I got my first bit of understanding one day when I was talking with my homie Amanda Seales. We were discussing the exploits of one of the many fuckbois we know when she sighed deeply and exhaled, "Brothas are damaged and they don't want to get any healing."

She wasn't talking *about me*, but the second she said it, I knew exactly what she was saying.

"Yes," I thought. "I am damaged. Incredibly damaged. And I need to heal."

That was a very important first step, admitting that I needed help.

It's a hard thing to do, especially when your public and professional life seems to be going so well.

It's even tougher when you've been raised to never show any weakness. Any sense of being overwhelmed. How could I share my struggle through a vocabulary I'd never learned to begin with?

Instead, I kept lying to myself. I closed ranks. I got paranoid. I was stressed because "haters" were out to get me. Or because my on-air competition was trying to bring me down.

It wasn't as far-fetched as it might sound. As many of you have probably seen on YouTube, one of my most envious competitors even sent a squad of goons to jump me outside of *The Breakfast Club* one morning. I managed to skedaddle before any real damage was done, but that's not the point.

It was convenient to point to all the professional drama for my unhappiness, but deep down I knew that wasn't really the case.

I just had to admit to myself that I was *miserable.*

Not only wasn't I happy, the more zeros in my bank account the more depressed I was; the success just made my anxiety worse. I was feeling more depressed than I ever had in my life.

One night, I told my wife how I was feeling. I told her I was thinking about going to talk to someone about what I'd been going through. She looked me dead in the eye.

"Baby," she told me, "just take your ass to therapy."

That was the final push that I needed.

I promised myself that I was going to forget about all the other "healing" I'd told myself would fix things, like drinking more water or going to the gym three times a week.

Those practices are great, but they weren't enough. No, this wasn't about my abs or looking like 50 Cent in '03. This was about real emotional healing.

I needed to have hard conversations: I needed to address with myself that I'd been raised wrong. That this version of me currently may have gotten me to a certain point, but if I wanted to go to the next level personally and professionally I needed to unlearn everything that clearly wasn't serving me anymore. I had to come to terms with the fact that I was a hurt person hurting other people.

Once I started going to therapy once a week, I was able to address the PTSD from my youth. I started to make sense of some of the things that had happened to me when I was young.

I found that going to therapy is like cleaning out a messy closet. Throwing out the things you don't need anymore (or maybe never did), so that you have room for the things that you *do*.

I was finally talking with myself (yes, with my therapist's help) instead of running from myself.

It's a process to which I'm still committed to this day. You can't unpack decades' worth of dysfunction and denial in a couple months, or even years. It's something that's going to be a part of my life forever.

But if for some reason, even after reading this, therapy still seems intimidating to you, I'd suggest another path to bring some peace into your life. Something that doesn't require a new doctor, a good medical insurance policy, or anyone else but yourself:

Meditation.

I'll admit that it wasn't something I thought I could do. It felt like my brain was too active to slow down and be silent.

But around the end of 2020, when the pandemic really shut everything down, I found myself doing it more and more often. We hear a lot of talk about what the pandemic cost us and how it changed things for the worse. But being at home and away from the distractions of my work and the city *forced* me to become more still for the first time. I was able to understand what quiet time really looks like and what peace really feels like.

That's why I'm fond of the saying "You can't heal what you don't reveal."

So whether it's through a conversation with a therapist, or becoming still by yourself through meditation, you need to find a way to reveal to *yourself* what's really going on in your mind.

Because until you do that, you're never going to heal from the trauma you've brushed up against in the world.

Let's discuss. . . .

CHAPTER 2

Put Some Respek on the Tortoise

This generation lacks a lot of things. A sense of direction (see what happens when you rely on Google Maps for everything?). Job prospects. Presidential candidates under the age of a hundred.

But what it lacks more than anything else is *patience.*

This generation loves being the hare, but doesn't have much respect for the tortoise. They're so eager to get out ahead of everyone, they don't even realize there's a whole race to run. And a lot of times they get halfway done and decide to chill. Then they see someone move out ahead of them and think, "What happened? This isn't fair."

I'll tell you what happened. You thought this was a sprint when it's really a marathon.

Apologies if I sound like a broken record (you know, one of those things we used to play music on) but *once again* I blame social media. On Instagram, we see the hiker at the top of the mountain. We see the picture of them smiling, taking in the majestic views. But we don't see the climb itself. We see the new home with the ocean views, but we don't see the years of hard work (nepo babies excluded) that went into saving up for that mortgage. We see someone post about losing thirty pounds, but they don't tell you they are an Ozempic Gold Medalist.

There's a reason we don't consider the journey. It is often difficult. It is lonely and uncomfortable. When my beige buddy Drake said,

"You wasn't with me shooting in the gym," that's exactly what he meant. He was in there all by his damn self. You gotta put up a thousand shots on your own before you get the chance to make that buzzer beater on national TV.

That's called the process. And the process is everything.

The great jazz musicians understood this. They had a term for the process called *woodshedding*, which was sometimes shortened to *shedding*. The idea was that before you could go on stage and perform in front of a crowd, or even behind closed doors with your peers, first you had to spend countless hours "in the woodshed," practicing alone. To achieve the right level of concentration, some of those guys would, no joke, go out into *the woods* to practice. Only after they'd put in all that work, all those hours of playing the same chords over and over and over again, would they then feel ready to perform in front of an actual crowd.

Some took it even further than that. Sonny Rollins, one of the all-time great saxophonists, used to live in New York City. Not a lot of woods to practice in. So during one stretch between 1959 and 1961, he'd spend over ten hours a day practicing by himself on the Williamsburg Bridge. Thousands of cars and people would go past him, and he would block it all out, lost in perfecting his craft.

Mind you, Rollins wasn't some unknown artist at that time either. He'd already played with several major jazz groups and had released a critically acclaimed album of his own. He could have decided he'd "made it," but he knew his competition would eat him up if he rested on his laurels. The culture of jazz demanded he keep shedding till he got to the place where he'd mastered his sound.

Compare that jazz culture to today's hip-hop culture. An aspiring rapper might make a few songs in their bedroom on their computer. Their friends tell them it's hot, so they release it. People listen to it on SoundCloud or TikTok. Maybe it goes viral. Then they get a record or distribution deal. Next thing you know, they're on stage performing in front of an actual crowd. And what does everyone say? "Man, this person has zero stage presence. Zero breath control. Get them out of here." And then their career is over almost as soon as it began.

But what did anyone expect? That rapper didn't spend hours in the park performing in front of an imaginary crowd, or in little bars and clubs around their hometown. They didn't spend hours rapping while they were running and jumping, so they'd be able to keep their breath as they moved around the stage. They didn't do any of that. They just thought, "OK, I'm hot. Put me out there."

And then they act surprised when their career stalls out just as it began.

Imagine an established rapper today putting in the hours that Sonny Rollins put in on that bridge. In fact, if there was an established rapper today putting in work on the Williamsburg Bridge, rapping at the top of their lungs for hours at a time over the roar of the traffic, let me tell you what would happen. Someone would walk along, see them rapping over the traffic and would film it. The video would go viral. And rather than celebrate an artist that was committed to their craft, people would clown them. They would treat them like they were Shep in *Above the Rim*, practicing dribbling without a ball. There would be memes and jokes all day.

But what there wouldn't be is a lot of folks going out there and practicing their own craft with the same level of intensity and dedication. Which is a shame. Because that's what it takes to not only make it to where you want to go, but actually stay there too.

I know this from firsthand experience. Clearly, early in my career, I wasn't the Charlamagne you see today. I wasn't on your TV screens, in your headphones, and for damn sure wasn't writing any books.

Not that I didn't want to do those things. I did. Very badly. But I hadn't put in enough work yet. And even though I had a dream, I had to do a lot of shedding before I could achieve it.

There were countless overnight on-air shifts from 12 a.m. to 5 a.m. or 2 a.m. to 6 a.m. Some people thought of them as "graveyards," but they are actually great shifts because you can really find yourself as a personality during those early-morning hours. That's where I found the freedom to try out different skits, characters, and approaches. Not all of them worked.

There are plenty of those experiments that would make me cringe if I listened to them today. In fact, I can't stand listening to most of the clips from earlier in my career. All I hear is the missteps, the blunders, the mistakes. But if I hadn't put in that work, I'd never be where I am today.

I'm still putting in that work. You might see a *Breakfast Club* interview go viral and it looks like I'm just sitting there asking people all kinds of random, wild stuff.

Just the opposite. No matter who is sitting in that seat across from me, I've tried to study them. I want to know who they are. I want to know what they've said. What they're about. What makes them tick. And, more importantly, I've given a lot of thought to what questions our *audience* wants answered. It's never just about me. And on the rare occasion that an interview happens at the last minute and I don't have time to do my normal prep, that's fine too. I'm naturally curious about other humans and appreciate the opportunity to get to meet someone new and learn about them on the fly, and I can do that skillfully because of the time I've put in over many years.

The lack of preparation and thoughtfulness is something that drives me a little nuts about podcasting. Don't get me wrong, I think podcasting overall has been tremendous for the audio industry. I am especially proud of my Black Effect podcast network. It's given a platform to so many Black voices that might otherwise have been overlooked. I'm confident when I look back at my career, it's going to stand as one of the most important things I did.

The issue is that the bar of entry to podcasting is so low that anyone can do it. All you need is a couple of mics, a quiet room, and a computer. You're ready to get in the game. That's great, but it doesn't mean everyone *should* be doing it. Yes, you and your friends might feel you have great conversations about what's on TV. Or sports. But just because your group chat is lit doesn't mean you are ready to make a show out of it. Especially when the majority of the time all you have to offer is a bunch of small talk!!

The Brilliant Idiots, the podcast I do with Andrew Schulz, feels like free-flowing conversation among friends. And in many ways it is. But think of all the woodshedding Andrew and I have done to make it feel that way. I've spent thousands and thousands of hours talking on the radio and on podcasts. Taking calls, making skits, reading the news, conducting interviews. Andrew has spent countless hours on stage, telling jokes, working the crowds, perfecting his delivery. Not to mention doing his own podcasts. When you hear a podcast like *The Brilliant Idiots*, you're hearing what we sound like after years and years of shedding. Not before.

I wonder how many people starting their own podcasts have put in that same time and practice. Sure, maybe it's not realistic to spend a decade working on your delivery before you launch a show, but have you taped a demo? Or five demos? Figuring out what works and what falls flat. Have you studied other successful podcasts to see what works for them? What you can borrow and apply in your own voice?

The answer, in too many cases, is no. Instead, most people just press record and start yapping away. And then wonder why they never build a larger audience.

This isn't just evident in the media. It's everywhere we look. Collectively we have no discipline. No willpower. We just want what we want, when we want it, and we want it now.

Granted, while I think the lack of patience has reached an all-time high, it's also an inherently human trait. Even back in the biblical days there were plenty of folks looking to take short cuts. Maybe they weren't spending enough time working on their sandal-making skills. Or slacking in their shepherding duties. I don't know. But I do know that in Proverbs 14:23 it's written: "There is profit in hard work, but mere talk leads to poverty." So obviously it was an issue back then too.

I know it's very easy to think in this day and age that success, money, material goods, and even love come quickly to people. I promise you, however, that the internet is filled with hares. And in case you forgot: the hare lost.

A lot of those material things, and even relationships, aren't going to be around for long.

I'm encouraging you to be the tortoise. To commit yourself to something, or someone, you're passionate about. Maybe it's not on the Williamsburg Bridge, or inside a radio studio, but commit yourself to creating that space for yourself where you can woodshed. Where you can put in the time and practice to become great at what you do. Where you have time to work out all the kinks and mistakes before you present your passion to the world.

When you put in that kind of work, I promise you it will be worth it in the end. As the Greek philosopher Aristotle put it, "Patience is bitter, but its fruit is sweet."

Let's discuss. . . .

CHAPTER 3

The Pursuit of Ignorance

A lot of useless small talk—often including straight-up lies—comes from people not being able to admit to their ignorance.

I'm not talking about ignorance of US foreign policy, macroeconomic trends, or ancient Chinese history.

Those are subjects we should be expected to be ignorant about—even though online everyone seems to be an expert on those things (or whatever else happens to be trending).

I'm talking about folks who are ignorant about basic, day-to-day life things, but carry themselves as if the opposite is true.

There's no way to calculate it, but I'm convinced that we're living in an era where there are many more stupid people than ever before.

"But Charlamagne," you might say, "are you saying modern Americans are dumber than, say, Medieval Europeans, who were eighty percent illiterate? Who used to determine whether a woman was a witch by tying her to a chair, throwing her into a pond, and seeing if she sunk or swam? Who believed that cleaning your body made you more likely to get sick? Dumber than that?"

Yes, dumber than stank, illiterate Europeans throwing "witches" into ponds. Because back then they didn't know a damn thing to do better. This generation does know better, yet still chooses stupidity. All the information is right there!! You don't need to travel to a library or even take a college class. The information is right there on your phone. People have all the facts but still choose to ignore them. Because they'd rather feed their feelings than do the research.

Don't believe me?

Just listen to the folks around you.

I'll be talking to someone—and not to sound too judgmental—but they won't be more than halfway through a five-minute sermon before I'm thinking, "Goddamn, this person really doesn't know what they're talking about."

I know you've felt the same way too.

One of my favorite movies is *Idiocracy*. It came out in 2006, and stars Luke Wilson, Maya Rudolph, Terry Crews, and Dax Shepard. It's about a soldier who takes part in this top secret, super-classified hibernation experiment, but they accidentally freeze him for too long and he wakes up five hundred years later. He finds himself in a dystopian society where commercialism has run rampant, mankind has embraced anti-intellectualism, and society is devoid of traits such as intellectual curiosity, social responsibility, justice, and human rights.

Do any aspects of the plot of *Idiocracy* sound familiar to you?

I hope so, because a lot of them sound familiar to me.

There's no question we're currently living in an idiocracy.

This new reality is not entirely our fault. We live in a world where technology has advanced at an unprecedented rate. When I grew up, if you wanted to make a phone call inside your house, you could only go as far as the cord stretched. (Which led to a lot of calls being made inside closets and bathrooms. Kids today can't even imagine that.)

Today, our phones are *everywhere*. And we barely even use them for talking. Instead, we've built our entire lives around apps. Some of those apps are great—Waze keeps me from getting lost, the health app lets me know how many steps I take each day, and I can use the iHeart or

Apple podcast app to check out my podcasts when I'm driving to work or hitting the gym. All things that add positive value to my life.

But the vast majority of apps aren't that valuable. Even worse, they're *addicting*.

If you consume anything on a consistent basis over time, it becomes a habit. And if you, like too many of us, spend the majority of your free time with your head down scrolling through TikTok, Twitter, Facebook, Instagram, and/or Snapchat, then you've got a *nasty* habit.

If you want proof of how bad your habit is, consider how hard it was to open up the pages of this book. It was probably a little difficult to focus at first, right? You probably told yourself you were going to crack this open a few times before you actually did. And since you did, you've probably felt the impulse to go "check" your phone more than a few times? (I mentioned this in the intro, but this is why I wanted these chapters to be short. Because I know what I'm up against. Hell, if I'm being honest, I've had a hard time writing this book because I've become so distracted by all the noise social media has created around me.)

It's not just books. You probably struggle to watch a documentary, a movie, or a TV show without picking up your phone to tweet through it. We can't even watch something without reading what other people think about the thing while we're watching it.

There are two problems with that. The first is that you're missing the essence of whatever that writer or director was trying to convey through their work. You're so busy trying to react to what other folks are thinking that you never fully understand whatever you're consuming.

The second is that by being so worried about everyone's opinion, you've lost the ability to come to your own conclusions. You've lost one of the key abilities that make you an actual human being—the ability to reason. You think you have an opinion, but in reality it's just a point of view that the internet has chosen for you. You don't have feelings or thoughts, you have a narrative that you've bought into.

Every time you open an app, what's one of the first things you check? What's *trending*. The Merriam-Webster dictionary defines a trend as "a current style or preference." But that's not how we use it anymore. The words "preference" and "style" convey a sense of choice, of optionality. But we treat "trending" as a fact now. Indisputable proof that someone, or something, has true value. What's the ultimate sign of validation you can give someone in this digital age?

"OMG, you're trending!"

It's like what being on the cover of *Time* magazine was like back in the day. The definitive sign that you've arrived and are important (of course it could also mean that you've messed up or even just plain old died).

But the subjects that are trending today aren't decided by a group of editors, or a panel of experts. No, they're decided by an algorithm. And that algorithm doesn't care—or even know—if a subject has value. It only cares about getting you to click on the subject.

Malcolm X once said the media's the most powerful entity on earth. Well, social media is the new media, so I ask the question: How much power does it have over you?

The truth is, you're being controlled by who you follow. Each person you follow is spewing out their own little gospel, their own doctrine. If the doctrine is coming from a trusted source, someone who vets their information and forms an intelligent opinion before popping off at the mouth, then I'd say you're doing OK. Or at least you're better off than most. Even then, you have to watch for the agenda, because nowadays everyone's got one.

A couple years ago Denzel Washington made an interesting comment about the news. He said, "If you don't read the newspaper, you're uninformed. If you do read it, you're misinformed."

Think about that comment for a second, because it relates to what I'm talking about with agendas. A newspaper, for the most part, is supposed to print the facts. A lot of times they do, but a lot of times they don't—or, how I interpret Denzel's quote is, they print the facts, but with a slant.

Now, if you think a newspaper, with millions of dollars invested in people who are paid to write and report the news, is getting it wrong sometimes, then what do you think these fools with access to social media accounts, YouTube channels, and blogs are doing to you? A lot of them are not even misinforming you. There is no slant. They're just straight-up lying.

My question is—what are those lies doing to you?

I can tell you what they've done to me—they've made me extremely anxious.

It's enhanced in my situation because some of the lies I read online are actually about me, which is an unnerving experience.

I've seen so many false stories about me that I've lost count. Still, to see someone write something about you with absolute clarity and conviction, even though *you know it is a lie*, will really mess with your head.

I try to stay sane by fully embracing the fact that a lie is a lie no matter how many people believe it, and the truth is the truth regardless of how many people *don't* believe it. One of the things I'm learning in life is people believe everything they hear online *except* for the truth!

I've also learned that people don't want the truth if it doesn't agree with the narrative they are trying to paint.

If a person doesn't like you, they are going to ride with anything that's against you and shoot down anything that paints you in a positive light. They will fertilize this lie every day, watering it and making sure it gets the proper sun, all in the hopes of watching that lie grow.

As Don Miguel Ruiz says, "The truth doesn't need you to believe it; the truth simply is, and it survives whether you believe it or not. Lies need you to believe them."

That reality—that the truth is often lost in people's beliefs—used to cause me a lot of stress. Not just relating to stories about myself, but seeing how much people were willing to overlook in order to support a narrative.

I finally learned to let go of that fear during the pandemic. One day I picked up Deepak Chopra's *Seven Spiritual Laws of Success*, which I try to flip through from time to time. On that particular day I read Law 6, "The Law of Detachment." In the chapter, Deepak writes,

> *In detachment lies the wisdom of uncertainty . . . in the wisdom of uncertainty lies the freedom from our past, from the known, which is the prison of past conditioning. And in our willingness to step into the unknown, the field of all possibilities, we surrender ourselves to the creative mind that orchestrates the dance of the universe.*

Ladies and gentlemen, I read those words during one of the scariest periods of my lifetime. It was the early days of the pandemic. Covid 19, coronavirus, That Bitch Rona— whatever you want to call it, it was all anyone could think of. There was no other conversation to be had (OK, except for *Verzuz*)—it was the number one trending topic for a year!

Prior to the pandemic, my therapist had been telling me to let go of things I can't control. My need to control everything—my career, my family, my health, my future—has always been one of the main sources of my anxiety.

In the pandemic, I had finally faced a fear that neither I—nor anyone else for that matter—had any control over. I'd finally met my match. For the first time in my life, I didn't have anywhere to go, anyone to see, or anything to do. All I could do was listen to the news 24/7 like everyone else.

After watching the endless press conferences from the President, health experts, and various politicians, I finally came to a conclusion on my own:

I Have No Idea What Is Going On. And Neither Does Anyone Else.

I didn't know if coronavirus was going to kill me or my family. I didn't know if I should shut my family up in our house or go about life like nothing was wrong. I didn't know if I should be first in line for a vaccine or just have faith in my own immune system.

I didn't have a good answer for any of those questions.

And you know what, I was perfectly fine with my ignorance.

And in that moment during the pandemic, I realized being able to admit that you don't have all the answers is one of the most freeing feelings in the world!! To not know and be absolutely comfortable with not knowing! Suddenly, for the first time in my life, I was ten toes down in the unknown and I didn't feel too shaky. In fact, I felt great!

I thought I'd be scared, but I was actually liberated from fear! The FOMO, or fear of missing out, is what keeps you glued to the TV, to social media, talk radio, podcasts, YouTube, and all of these various platforms.

I had been looking for one of the so-called experts to reassure me, to tell me everything was going to be all right. But for the first time in my life, I could clearly see that there weren't any experts to reassure me. Nobody had a real handle on what was going on.

Obviously a lot of lunatics rushed into that vacuum. The people who wanted us to believe that Bill Gates was using coronavirus to install human trackers, that 5G cell towers were to blame for the virus, that coronavirus would usher in the New World Order, and a personal favorite, that the pandemic was a government effort to force people to stay home so they could save the world from devil-worshipping sex traffickers, who included the likes of Oprah Winfrey and Tom Hanks. Whew!

I can't even fully blame those folks. As Bruce Lee once put it very simply, "People fear what they don't understand."

And there was such a fundamental lack of understanding at that moment, the resulting fear was almost inevitable.

Why do you think the people who thought Tom Hanks and Oprah were out there eating babies were so argumentative and combative? Because they needed you to believe what they believed so they could feel more comfortable and less afraid. Groupthink is a powerful security blanket. I love my weighted blanket because you know what it does for me? It helps me ease my anxiety.

That's what conspiracy theories and misinformation did for a lot of people in 2020.

But unlike me with my weighted blanket, I don't think they felt any better after running with those lies and untruths. If anything, I suspect they got more anxious and depressed because they knew deep down they were wrapping themselves up in lies.

When you're facing the unknown, it's OK to say, "I don't know nothing." And then sit comfortably in that lack of knowledge.

Let's all try to learn that there is nothing wrong with not knowing. In fact, there is incredible power in embracing what you don't know, especially when you can't control the outcome of the situation anyway.

When you let go of what you think something is, or what you think something should be, and just allow yourself to BE—man, that is true happiness.

Let's discuss. . . .

CHAPTER 4

Father Time

One of the most important conversations in my life took place Thanksgiving weekend in 2018. I had just released my second book, *Shook One: Anxiety Playing Tricks on Me.*

Even though writing a book about my mental health struggles had been very cathartic, there were still a few issues in my life that felt unresolved.

And my relationship with my father was at the top of that list.

I had been pretty candid about my father in the book. I wrote that I loved my Pops and at the end of the day I considered him a good father. But I was also clear about the fact that he was an absolutely terrible husband and that, despite hours and hours of therapy, I still had a lot of resentment over how he treated my mother. To make it even more complicated, I also blamed his example as contributing to the piss-poor way I grew to treat women I was in relationships with, especially my own wife.

When it comes to women and relationships, my father has had me on a roller coaster since I was a kid. I first found out he was cheating on my mom when I was around seventeen years old. I was rightfully indignant and confronted him. In my mind, once he saw how upset I was, he would make things right immediately.

My father had no interest in doing that. Instead, he just gaslit me.

"What am I apologizing for?" he asked me incredulously when I demanded he tell my mother he was sorry. Then he looked me dead in the eye and said, "So you've only got one girlfriend, huh? One day, when you're older, you'll understand."

That immediately took the wind out of my sails. I had started the conversation furious at my father and ended it mad at myself. My father had tricked me into thinking the idea of monogamy and faithfulness was laughable. For suckers. And my father had definitely not raised me to be a sucker. I felt compelled to prove to him I was a chip off the old cheating block.

Remember, this was my first male role model. That's normal for any son. But my father was something of a living legend in Moncks Corner. He had a hand in almost everything. Construction. Selling fish. Owning a club. Selling a little coke here and there too. He liked to wear bright colors. He had a Jheri curl. There was simply no way you could live in Moncks Corner and not know who Larry McKelvey was. My entire existence centered around being Larry's son.

The man was a straight-up superhero to me.

So when he gaslit me, he lit me up *good*.

I spent a long time trying to prove to myself that I was just as much of a player as my old man. That I also operated by my own rules. That being tied down to one woman was something for squares and suckers.

To be fair, my father wasn't the only person putting that poison in my ear. I had another mentor in the Low Country area, a person who shall remain nameless because I must protect the guilty. He told me, "Listen, son, every man should have two women." He didn't even bother trying to justify the concept, he just stated it as fact. As if he were explaining how to fix a car engine.

That advice from two separate male role models really screwed me up. Can I entirely lay the blame for my behavior at their feet? Of course not. But those attitudes certainly made it easier for me to adopt the culture of unfaithfulness.

I was an active participant in that culture for many years. Like I said, I didn't understand their advice, I over-stood!

I took cheating to levels that my father never imagined back in small-town South Carolina. My father had one or two women stashed on the side. By the time I'd started to make it big in radio, I probably had a starting five. If my father had just been breaking the speed limit, I was going a hundred miles per hour.

There are a lot of stupid, shameful memories, but one that really stands out was a time I was staying at the SLS Hotel in Los Angeles. One morning I had a young lady sleeping in my bed when I suddenly saw my wife FaceTiming me. I'd told her I was planning to go to the gym after I woke up. Not lying in bed with someone else.

When the other woman saw the phone ringing, she looked at me and said, "I'll just hide under the covers."

Now, any sane person would have said, "No, it's time for you to go." And then waited till she was gone to call back his wife.

But not me.

I waited for her to get under those covers and then I picked up my wife's call.

Looking back on it, what the hell was I thinking? Why did I trust that woman not to make a sound while I spoke to my wife? Why was she there in the first place?

Like I said, I was completely out of control.

It took me a very long time to get that sort of behavior in check.

It started when I began to realize I was becoming just like *him*.

Yes, I'd surpassed my father in terms of income. I'd seen more of the world. Met some of my heroes. Become a hero to others. I was a big fish in the ocean, not just in a small pond.

But I was about to lose what was most important to me—my family—the same way he'd lost his.

My breakthrough finally came when I started therapy.

I realized I had a tremendous amount of resentment toward him. I resented that he made me think I was a loser because I wasn't cheating. I resented that he sent me out into the world with a terrible attitude toward relationships. And of course, I still resented what he'd done to my mother.

As I started peeling back the layers of dysfunction, miscommunication, and gaslighting that defined our relationship, I just started crying.

The more I examined our relationship, the more I began to find the words to express my pain. I was mad at my father for things he never taught me and furious at him for the wrong things he *did* teach me. I began to wonder, "Do I hate this man?"

For years he had been the planet my life revolved around, but I started to feel like I never wanted to talk to him again.

Then came that Thanksgiving weekend. My father called and left a message to say he'd just read *Shook One* and wanted to talk.

Right away, my head started spinning. My father was not the type of guy to just want to "talk." My father might give directions, or even a lecture, but just talk? No, that wasn't him.

Plus, I could hear the emotion in his voice. He was in his feelings. And I thought I knew why. It wasn't just because of what he'd read about himself in my book. My cousin, who my father was close with, had just completed suicide at the age of twenty-five. It was his fourth attempt at taking his own life. I knew my father was hurting.

When we finally got on the phone, my father told me that between reading the book and my cousin's suicide, he'd realized some things. In his mind, *I* was the one who'd always had things together while *he'd* been struggling.

He was so caught up in his own problems that he'd never truly seen what I was going through. But, he wanted me to know, he could relate. And then he told me something I'd never known about him.

It turns out that my father had been dealing with severe depression and anxiety most of his life. He was going to therapy several times a week and was on multiple medications. At one point things had gotten so bad that he'd had to check into a mental health rehab. He'd even wanted to kill himself, but hadn't because he didn't want to hurt his children.

This was all news to me. Yes, I'd known that things weren't always right with my father growing up. I could sense it. He'd been to jail. There was a period where he used to talk about the Devil looking to get him. During that time he'd sleep with a pistol under his pillow. I knew things were off.

But in a small town like Moncks Corner, talking about the Devil and sleeping with a pistol doesn't seem all that crazy. A lot of folks do. Just like a lot of folks ended up in jail. It almost seemed like par for the course.

After I spoke with my father, I immediately called up my mother. "Did you know Dad was going through all that?" I asked.

"Well, I knew about the medication and the therapy," she replied. "But I thought he was just playing crazy to get a check."

What my mother was referring to was what we would call the "crazy checks." Basically, if you had mental health issues and the doctors couldn't properly diagnose it, the government would put you on disability and pay you a monthly stipend. My mother figured being "crazy" was just another one of my father's many hustles.

When I got off the phone with her, I was frustrated that all that had gone on and no one had ever talked to me about it. But that frustration quickly gave way to an incredible sense of freedom.

I realized right then and there this basic truth: that my superhero was also a man. Someone who had never gotten the chance to heal from his own traumas. My father had filled my head up with small talk over all those years because he was too ashamed to be honest with his then teenage son and tell him what he was actually dealing with himself.

I realized my father was just a man who, like so many men in my community, was overwhelmed by his environment.

I had to give him a lot of grace. He was doing the best he could with what he had. My generation is the first that's had the luxury of healing; my father's generation was just trying to survive.

But by not being the best version of himself, he didn't allow me and my siblings to become the best versions of ourselves either. We've had to put in a lot of work to make up for what we lost by not having honest conversations in our family. By not being honest about what everyone was going through.

That's why I'm trying to make sure I have those conversations with my kids, no matter how painful or awkward they might be. Those talks can be hard, but they are worth it.

I'm really encouraged by this generation when I see iconic artists like Kendrick Lamar put out a song like "Father Time."

I got daddy issues, that's on me
Lookin' for, 'I love you,' rarely empathizin' for my relief . . .

— — —

That was such a powerful record. It's been rare to hear Black men express that pain and trauma, but I'm hoping it becomes the norm for this generation. Men, especially Black men, don't talk about the dynamic between them and their fathers enough.

But those are the conversations you *must* have.

Let's discuss. . . .

CHAPTER 5

Evolutionary Revolutionary

I like to say that I'm the perfect blend of ratchetness and righteousness.

What I mean by that is, like most people, I'm complex.

There are parts of me that embrace the ratchet: The messy. The dramatic. The potentially problematic.

Like when I was sniffing J.Lo's chair after she sat in it. (Look, I promised my listeners I would, so I had to keep my word!)

I've also had my righteous moments: Like when I hold my annual free Mental Wealth Expo in NYC every year or my annual bookbag and turkey giveaways in South Carolina. Not to mention my Ford Family Endowed Scholarship Fund (Ford is my mother's maiden name) that I set up at my mother's alma mater, South Carolina State University. I'm fully aware that to whom much is given, much is required. I definitely try to do my part.

My issue is that for many years, I was more comfortable sharing my ratchet side with the world.

It started when I was very young. As I've said before, I was a nerd growing up. A kid with a fanny pack and Coke-bottle glasses. I cared deeply about doing well in school. My mother was an English teacher and my dad always stressed the importance of education, so I wanted to make them proud.

And for a while, I did.

But when I was in sixth grade, a bunch of kids, many of them my cousins, started to take issue with my nerdy, academic ways. They said I was acting "white." They said I thought I was better than them because I was in the class where the majority of kids were white.

In retrospect, I can see that they were just projecting their own insecurities onto me. They were worried that they couldn't keep up in school. They didn't have a parent who encouraged their success.

To deflect from their insecurities, they created a narrative that there was something wrong with *me*. That I was weird. That I wasn't "Black enough." So that's when the bullying started. Harassing me before and after school. If I walked past them, they'd push me and knock my glasses off my face.

Looking back at those days, I can see now that it wasn't that serious. It was the type of harassing and bullying a lot of kids go through. Hell, the type of bullying that I'd later put plenty of kids through myself. But at the time it felt like my world was collapsing. These were my friends, my cousins. The kids I'd spent most of my time with. And now they'd turned on me. Every day felt like torture. And I didn't have anywhere to turn for help—if I would have told my father I was getting bullied, he would have made me go square up with everyone who was bullying me.

My father was not trying to hear that I was being bullied, because that would have meant I was being a punk. Why was that so bad? Imagine if you are a man in a small town where everyone knows each other. If your son is bullying my son, that means your son is "tough" and my son is a punk. A father like mine could take that as an indictment of himself. Especially if he considered the other father a punk. Imagine that, growing up thinking someone is a punk only to have that punk's son bully your son. No, I could definitely not be a punk in my father's eyes.

So, in order to survive, I created a character. He didn't have a name yet, but this character was on a mission to match those kids on every antisocial, anti-academic, and even criminal level. I was tired of being bullied. If they valued being bad, I would be even *worse*.

My new character continued to develop as I grew into a teenager. He got into selling drugs, committing petty crimes, and acting arrogant around women. My true self started fading further and further into the background.

Unfortunately, my plan worked. Those kids might have picked on Lenard, but they left this new guy alone. Encouraged by the results, I continued to double down on that negative energy.

It wasn't until I was in *night school* getting my diploma that this new character finally developed a name:

Charlamagne Tha God.

I've told this story before, but for the people who are new here, let me tell you how I came up with *that*. At the time I was going by the name Charlie, because I was selling drugs and wanted the fiends to call me by a fake name when they pulled up. Then one day I was reading a history book (after smoking a blunt) and saw that Charlemagne was French for Charles the Great. I was already going by Charlie, so I decided to transform myself from a dope dealer named Charlie into Charlamagne.

I was also studying the teachings of the Five Percenters (an offshoot of the Nation of Islam), so I added "Tha God" into the mix.

My new name reflected both sides of my personality. Yes, it was a nod to my ratchet side—an offbeat moniker inspired by smoking too much weed and my need to disguise my identity from fiends I was selling to.

But it also reflected my righteous ambitions. I had read about the historical King Charlemagne being a great man, someone who was a leader and had changed the course of the world in his time. Someone I aspired to be like.

As I grew older, I became more and more invested in the character. When I first got on the radio in South Carolina, it allowed me to be way more outlandish and aggressive than I often really felt inside. The geeky little kid with glasses and a fanny pack who just wanted to read books? He got buried under a lot of layers of bravado.

My character gave me the confidence to take chances. To challenge my competitors. To ask questions and give the kind of opinions other radio jocks wouldn't.

By the time I landed on *The Breakfast Club*, it was hard for me to separate myself from that character.

My persona was absolutely resonating with listeners. As more and more articles were written about me, the person I kept getting compared to was Howard Stern. Back then, Howard was still known as a shock jock, someone who would do anything for ratings. The guy who might throw baloney at a naked woman's ass, berate members of his staff on-air, or verbally attack celebrities. I can see now that Howard was already beginning his evolution into the thoughtful, insightful personality he's celebrated as today, but I was too blinded by the attention I was receiving to notice. All I could see was the ratings his outrageous behavior seemed to have generated. If Howard had parlayed being a shock jock into being the King of All Media, then I was going to follow the same path.

I created even more characters. I dubbed myself the "Prince of Pissing People Off" and the "Ruler of Rubbing You the Wrong Way." Then I set out to earn those titles.

The truth is, I was afraid not to. I needed the character in order not only to thrive, but to *survive*. Or at least that's how I perceived it. And the only way I could deliver any righteousness was through leaning hard into the ratchet. Put the medicine in the candy. But what happens when a kid gets too much candy? They get sick.

That's what happened to me. Subconsciously, I started pandering.

I found myself for a brief period saying the things I knew would get my audience riled up, not because I necessarily believed what I was saying, but because I craved the attention that *The Breakfast Club* seemed to get from those moments.

It was a very dangerous mindset to be in. I had become a caricature of myself.

At a certain point, I wasn't even sure who I was anymore. Was I the boisterous radio guy who radiated "I don't give a fuck energy"? Or was I still that shy, geeky kid who wanted to retreat into the corner of any room he was in and just observe?

Even as I grew more and more outwardly successful, those questions kept gnawing at me.

Finally, with the help of therapy, I came up with an answer:

I had to evolve.

Not into Howard Stern. Or any other media figure.

Into myself.

Into the person I already was, but had been afraid to share with the world.

I've always been well rounded. I was a kid who grew up on both Judy Blume *and* Mobb Deep. Who was just as comfortable hanging out with his grandmother talking about God as he was hanging out in the trap with the homies selling crack.

I just had to learn how to share *all* of myself with the world.

I had to tell myself that even though the public might love Charlamagne, they'd learn to love Lenard the same way too.

Frankly, I'd be disappointed in myself if I hadn't begun to show more sides of myself. If I'd stayed stuck in the same rowdy character I developed as a teenager.

If that's the price of success and fame, then y'all can keep it. I feel much more rewarded being able to grow and share my evolution with the world.

A character is constricting. Evolution is freedom.

Muhammad Ali once said, "If a person is doing the same thing at fifty that they were at twenty, that just means that they wasted thirty years of their life." I subscribe to that theory.

I'm forty-five as I write this. Why would anyone expect me to act the same way I did, or have the same conversations that I had, when I was twenty-five? If I did that, either I'd have been wasting a lot of time on this planet, or I wouldn't be authentic. Neither is an acceptable option for me.

I've always viewed evolution as a positive part of people's personalities. Books like *The Autobiography of Malcolm X* and *Message to the Blackman in America* by Elijah Muhammad had a tremendous impact on me as a young man. As did a book I read when I was locked up in jail called *From Niggas to Gods* by Akil.

Yes, these books were about the communal challenges faced by African-Americans in a racist society. But they were also about something equally as important—*personal evolution*. Each provided a blueprint on how folks can grow. How Malcolm X could go from a pimp and drug addict to one of the most inspiring leaders of the twentieth century. How the Nation of Islam can take the worst of us and mold them into the best of us. How, as the title of Akil's book suggests, a group of ostracized people can transform themselves into the highest form of beings.

You would think America would embrace these kinds of narratives. That as a society, we would champion anyone who shows signs of transforming themselves into something better than what they were.

Instead, I see the opposite mentality developing.

Our conversations, especially online, have turned incredibly judgmental. There's very little room for correction where someone was once wrong. For making a joke that was more hurtful than funny. For having a take that didn't age well. There doesn't seem to be any room to change your perspective.

It makes me ask, "When did we decide it's not OK for people to make mistakes? When did we decide that it's not OK for people to grow?"

I find this type of intolerance very scary. And to be clear, I'm not looking for any sympathy for myself here. I'm very comfortable in my evolution and I don't feel like I need to apologize for how I came across in the past.

I know who I was and I know who I've become. And who I hope to be down the road. I'm very comfortable with that dynamic. My growth isn't dependent on other people's approval.

But I worry for people growing up now, especially teenagers like my kids. When we see that anxiety, depression, and even suicide rates are so high with young people today, we have to ask why. I truly believe a big factor is that we're telling them they have to be perfect.

Not just in how they look and what they have, but how they *think*.

Try to think back to how you felt at that age. Where every breakup, every argument, every reprimand felt like the end of the world.

Now try to imagine being a kid in an environment where you're being told that it really is the end of the world. Because that's what "cancel" means:

The end.

That's incredibly frightening for these kids, let alone adults.

And it's why I'm going to promote evolution over termination. Growth over censure.

Look, I know how I've evolved. And I know how people around me have changed too.

I knew folks like Jeezy and T.I. back when we all were in our early twenties. They were not the same men they are today. Back then, a lot of folks saw them as thugs. As negative influences.

Two decades later, they're pillars of their community. Respected elders in the culture. And I've seen it happen so many other times. Which is why when I meet a Sexyy Red or a Kodak Black today, I try not to judge them too strongly. Because I know no matter where they are as twenty-year-olds, they can be in a completely different place as forty-year-olds.

My role now is not to encourage outrageousness, or to purposely piss people off. It's to encourage evolution. When I meet folks, on the radio or out in the world, I want to have real conversations. Not scandalous small talk. I'm only looking at them as human beings.

Human beings that might have started out in one place, but have the potential to go somewhere else.

I'd encourage you to look for that same potential in the people you meet.

And more importantly, in *yourself.*

We are all works in progress. The more we can embrace that process, and let go of the unnecessary judgment and holier-than-thou attitudes, the quicker we'll all be able to evolve into the best versions of ourselves.

Let's discuss. . . .

CHAPTER 6

DEI (Not That One)

There's been a lot of debate in this country lately about DEI, or diversity, equity, and inclusion. You know, corporate initiatives that look to promote "the fair treatment and full participation of all people."

Seems like the type of concept that we should all be able to agree on, but Republicans have latched on to it as their next political buzz phrase, next to CRT, death panels, welfare moms, the migrant caravan (that sounds kinda dope actually), and any other number of made-up controversies they throw around when it's time to vote. But right now I want to talk about another DEI.

This one, however, doesn't stand for diversity, equity, and inclusion.

It stands for delusion, entitlement, and idiocracy!

And its symptoms are impacting young people today in unprecedented ways.

I know, I know. Every generation thinks the generation that came after them is soft.

Didn't pay their dues.

Don't realize how easy they have it.

Haven't faced any real struggle.

You've probably heard this classic bar from your own parents (hell, I'm a proud parent of four and I use it all the time): "Back in my day we had to . . ."

You can fill in the blank.

Walk to school barefoot for ten miles. Pluck roaches out the cereal box. Share one pair of pants with three brothers. Survive winters, snotty nose with no coats. Didn't have enough toilet paper, so we had to use the newspaper instead. (Basically every struggle Ghostface describes in "All That I Got Is You.")

There's no generation that didn't think *they* had it the hardest.

But having said that, there is zero question that young people today have it easier than the generations that came before them.

I don't care if you're twenty-eight, forty-eight, or sixty-eight years old. You know I'm right.

One of the sayings we all grew up with was "actions speak louder than words."

But this might be the first generation where words now speak louder than actions.

I'm referring to how this generation lives online first, where words and images have become more important than making actual contributions to the "real world."

Growing up, my father would always tell me, "Ain't no future in fronting." His point was you can run your mouth and BS about a situation for a very long time, but eventually you have to put some sort of plan into effect.

Well, I don't know if my father's words ring true anymore, because this generation seems to think the front is more important than the facts.

Folks use social media to promote what seem to be incredible lifestyles. Perfectly lit shots from picturesque locations. Tulum. Jamaica. Paris. On the Jet Skis by that rusty-ass boat in Turks and Caicos. All with some Drake lyrics for a caption. The kind of posts that have hundreds, sometimes thousands, of people telling them how beautiful they look. How incredible their lives must be.

Never mind that the ocean view is taken from the balcony of an Airbnb they can only afford for one night. And even then, that's with five friends splitting the bill. Or even worse, rented via a credit card number they scammed.

Never mind that their bank account is in the red and they're asking people at work for loans so they can pay the rent on the apartment they actually live in.

In the eyes of the world, the "pretenders" have already made it. And even worse, they're setting the standard.

Which makes a lot of other people in their age bracket think they deserve to be living that sort of lifestyle too.

I believe the internet influencers are where a lot of today's entitlement comes from. If you're in your early twenties, or even thirties, and a lot of your peers seem to be spending the weekends on the beach in the Caribbean, or working out of a café in Amsterdam, it's understandable that you'll start to believe you *deserve* to be living a similar lifestyle.

So when your current situation doesn't allow you to run off to chill in Dubai at the drop of a dime, you start to feel like somebody's doing you wrong. When the pay at your job doesn't leave you with enough to have a nice apartment *and* spend weekends jet-setting outside the country, it feels like someone must be holding you back. That you deserve more than you currently have.

I struggle to understand that mentality. I never thought that way in my twenties. Or any age for that matter.

When I moved to New York City in 2010 to host *The Breakfast Club*, it was the most money I had ever made in radio: $125k a year. When I'd been in New York for *The Wendy Williams Show*, I wasn't even paid at all for the first year and a half. Not a dime. When I did start getting paid, after working for free, it was $75k a year. I certainly didn't have an apartment of my own. I certainly wasn't thinking about Caribbean vacations. I didn't even have a passport yet! I damn sure wasn't thinking about dining out at cool restaurants. Who was going to pay for that? All I was thinking about was how I could keep honing my craft and continue to reach a bigger audience.

All my energy was focused on the substance of what I wanted to create. Style didn't matter.

Especially life*style*.

Even after I landed the *Breakfast Club* gig, my lifestyle stayed basic. Once I could finally afford my own place, some friends suggested that I move into the Prospect Towers in Hackensack, New Jersey. It was a cool complex, but far from glamorous. (And far from my gig in Manhattan too.) No fancy lobby. No heated swimming pool or valet parking. Just a solid apartment building. In an affordable area.

And there were other successful folks there. Rosci Diaz, who was hosting *106 & Park* at the time, stayed there. My good sister Alesha Renee, who was on MTV's *Guy and Girl Code* at the time, lived there, as did several members of the New York Jets and Giants. Nobody was worried about their online brand. Everyone was focused on their career. Doing their job. They just wanted a safe and warm place to lay their head when they finally got home at night. The Prospect Towers fit the bill.

Back in the day, no one felt the need to put on a front when they were just starting out. I met so many current stars on their way up and they all shared a single trait: they were laser focused on THE WORK. Not how they looked.

I met T.I. in 2002. He didn't have jewelry on. Or gold teeth. He was in between record deals because he had just been dropped from LaFace. He came to the radio station the Big DM in Columbia, South Carolina, with just a gray Champion hoodie. His song "24's" was on a white-label CD. Same with Gucci Mane. First time I met him, he was sporting jean shorts and a red polo shirt, with a red bandanna tied around his head. He looked like he had just stepped fresh out the trap (which he probably had).

I remember Ludacris when he was first making the transition from being a radio DJ to a rapper. He stopped by Z93 Jamz in Charleston, South Carolina, and he even ran the board during his own interview. There was no ego, no expectation of anyone handing these guys anything. They were all hungry and on their grind.

When I reflect on the humbleness and focus I witnessed on my way up, I don't know where this broad sense of entitlement comes from today.

No, I'm lying.

It comes from social media. It goes back to what I just said at the top of the chapter. Everybody wants to front and pretend.

Hey, I get it. Sometimes you need to present the lifestyle you want to the world before you truly achieve it.

Or, in other words, fake it till you make it. You turn out to be what you pretend to be. Manifestation. *The Secret.* We've heard it.

The problem is, a lot of kids are faking out themselves in the process. For my NBA fans reading this, imagine Allen Iverson, Kyrie Irving, or Ja Morant crossing themselves up in the mirror and breaking their own ankles. That's exactly what this generation is doing.

Just because you've created the *illusion* that you're making money doesn't mean that you also *deserve* to make money. Just because you *believe* you will get to the goals you've set out doesn't mean you've already gotten there.

Let me tell you what you deserve when you're fresh out of school and entering the workplace.

You deserve good health. (And health care. Though good luck with that in America.)

You deserve (some) peace of mind. As much as humanly possible.

You deserve to be able to follow your dreams without being harassed, abused, or discriminated against because of your race, gender, or physical ability.

You deserve to know that if you keep God first, stay humble, and keep working, then you'll have a *chance* to advance.

And that's about it.

What you don't *deserve* is a six-figure salary. Or "me time." Or leaving your office before your boss who's been there for twenty years leaves. Or (my favorite) to be "heard."

I witness this entitled mentality almost every day. Just recently there was someone in their twenties who was complaining to me that they hadn't advanced to an executive level yet. "I've been doing this for four years!" the young person told me in complete frustration.

I had to laugh. To these kids today, four years is a lifetime. My mother taught in the same school district for over thirty years and never made over $30,000. Four years? That's just getting your feet wet. You haven't even jumped in the deep end yet.

Also, keep in mind that when this person complained about not getting promoted after four years, we were in the middle of a historically bad media market. Companies in TV, film, audio, and streaming had been laying people off by the hundreds. Sometimes thousands. There were so many qualified, hungry, unemployed people out there who would have happily taken the job for four months, forget about four years!

I'm not saying that young people should sell themselves short. Or stop advocating for themselves. But you can't even begin to have those conversations unless you've put in real work. Where it's clear that you've outworked everyone around you. And even then, you don't deserve more. You've just created more of a case for yourself.

I have seen so many people literally talk themselves out of tremendous opportunity and growth by believing that they should be given more than they were getting.

There's a situation in particular that still boggles my mind to this day. I had a homie who worked with me for years. They were good at their job, but I was overpaying them. Wildly. But I was cool with it. They were my people, had had my back in situations, and I wanted them to feel secure.

But even after getting extravagantly (I'm talking six figures) over-paid for years, they still felt like they deserved more. In their mind, they couldn't just live in any old place. They couldn't drive just any old thing. They were meeting celebrities through the job, but in their mind they deserved to become a celebrity too. And to look, live, and eat like one too. They felt that I was somehow getting over on them.

Eventually, I had to let the person go. More so than money, it was about poor judgment. But after it happened, Humble Lukanga, my financial advisor, called me up. "I know you two were tight. But you were paying them way too much money," he told me. "They're never going to be able to make that kind of money again."

Humble said he'd known I was overpaying since the beginning. "But I never said anything because I know that's your friend," he explained. "Besides, I've got clients that have ten of those kinds of friends. You only had one. I wasn't tripping, but thank God that expense is gone."

That kind of talk might sound cold, but that's what everyone is up against in life. No matter where you work, or who you work for, there's a Humble somewhere looking at the bottom line. And that person doesn't care if you feel like you deserve more. They care about what you're bringing to the situation. And if that isn't enough, then your days might be numbered.

You can say, "That's not fair," and while that might technically be true, when has any job or career or situation ever truly been fair? Never.

I've been in plenty of situations that weren't fair. It wasn't "fair" that I didn't get paid on *The Wendy Williams Show* even though I was on the air every day. It wasn't "fair" that my voice wasn't "heard" when decisions were being made off the air. A lot of things happened in that situation that weren't "fair."

Were those moments frustrating? Sure. But did they ever stop me from working my hardest on that show? Absolutely not.

My position on that show was an opportunity. A major one at that. And a major opportunity to prove myself has always been worth more to me than salary. Or even fairness. What have I always told y'all? You have to recognize opportunity even when there's not a paycheck attached to it.

Your focus should always be on creating and then capitalizing on opportunity.

I can't be complaining about what I see as a lack of compensation. Or respect.

There are exceptions to this rule, as there are to any. Whenever there's the presence of sexual or racial discrimination, then yes you have to stand up for yourself and call it out. But when that's not the case, you have to expect less and work for more.

Why? Because that's the way things are and the way things always will be.

Now, I know some of you "entreprenegroes" are out there saying, "That won't be me, I'll work for myself!! I'm my own CEO!" I respect that, but here's some breaking news:

WORKING FOR YOURSELF IS SOOOOO MUCH HARDER!!!!

All the pressures and expectations and concerns you have working for someone else increase times one hundred when you're doing it by yourself, working without a net. And believe me, when you're working for yourself, you realize very quickly that "entitled" isn't a word that fits in your vocabulary anymore. All you can do is put the work in. And then put some more work on top of that.

Let's discuss. . . .

CHAPTER 7

The Language of Politics Is Dead

I want to talk about one of the biggest conversations we need to have as a country:

How tired we are of the way politicians talk to us.

We've been saying this forever, but we've really hit an inflection point.

Nobody—Blue or Red, white or black, man or woman, young or old—wants to hear the "normal" political voice anymore.

You know the voice I'm talking about. The one that's safe. That's scared to take any chances. That's afraid to address the elephant in the room even though everyone can see it.

Remember when the parents used to talk in *Peanuts* and all Charlie Brown would hear was "wah wah waaaa"? Well, that's what all Americans hear when politicians open their mouths these days.

The difference is that in the past the public didn't have many options on how to receive information. Almost every message—from politicians to teachers to newscasters—was delivered in a safe, non-inflammatory, non-problematic, perfectly pronounced voice.

The internet killed all that. People have gotten used to hearing ideas—and not just news, but all topics—in *authentic* voices. In the kind of voices that get used around kitchen tables. In barbershops. In beauty salons. On corners. Even after a couple of drinks.

And we like it.

Like a dog who's gotten a taste of red meat, we're not interested in the canned stuff anymore. Give us that steak!

The language of politics is dead. If you've never watched the film *Bulworth* starring Warren Beatty, Halle Berry, and Don Cheadle, do yourself the biggest favor and go watch so you can see what Democratic politics is missing.

Some of the politicians out there already understand this. And a lot of them seem to be Republican.

They seemed to have gotten the memo that folks aren't interested in sanitized political discussions anymore. I happen to disagree with a lot of what Republicans are talking about, but there's no debating they're getting results from the authentic, less restrained voice they use in getting their messages out there.

It feels like the kind of voices I'm used to hearing in my own life. I think Marjorie Taylor Greene is a Whole Fools Market, and an actual menace to society, but I bet she sounds like most of her constituents. It played a major role in how she got elected in the first place.

The Democrats, on the other hand, don't seem to know how to talk to their constituents. Everything that comes out of their mouths, even the things I personally agree with on a factual level, start to sound inauthentic to me. They need to start for the first time ever having real conversations with people.

And I know that they're capable of it. Do you know why? Because behind the scenes, I hear how they speak.

I can't divulge too many details, but I've spoken to Hillary Clinton on and off the air. On the air, she was a politician. Even on *The Breakfast Club*, where politicians say they're going to "lay down their guard" and "get real," Hillary was still measured. The one time she went off script was when she told me she had hot sauce in her purse and I asked her, "Is this going to be one of those times people say you are pandering to Black people?" Her answer was "Is it working?"

Some people criticized Hillary for that response, but I liked it. I thought it was very honest. And it gave a glimpse of who she really is.

I've talked to Hillary behind the scenes, and trust me, she's a real human. Again, I can't get into specifics, but suffice it to say she really does have a great "muthafucker"; the way she says "muthafucker" might even rival Samuel Jackson.

I found it refreshing. Because that's how people talk. If anything, Hillary should have shared even more of that side of her with the public. I think if she had, it would have helped her tremendously in the 2016 presidential election.

That's because Donald Trump is someone who completely understands the power in not speaking safe. Not that I want my politicians to be as reckless and dangerous as Trump, but I do want them to tap into some of his *perceived* authenticity. (I'll never understand how a bunch of salt-of-the-earth white folks decided that a guy born into the lap of luxury with a silver spoon in his mouth was one of them. . . .)

My issue with Hillary has also been my issue with Kamala Harris. When I endorsed her in 2020, it was because of my *private* conversations with her, not because of the persona she presents in public.

The vice president needs to talk to the world the way she talks with me. Or her sister, Maya. It might go against protocol, it might make a few waves initially, but I promise you Kamala Harris will be a much more effective—and popular—politician if she goes off script and starts sharing more of herself.

I'm far from alone in feeling this way. I know this because as soon as I started talking publicly about the lack of plain talk in politics, I started connecting with a much larger audience.

I spoke about it on *The Daily Show*. I spoke about it on CNN, where I said, "The Democrats suck at messaging."

And the more I spoke about it, the more I started getting approached by people who just wanted to thank me for giving voice to one of their frustrations. White folks, Black folks, Asian folks, Jewish folks—they're all telling me the same thing: We appreciate your common sense. We appreciate that you are telling these politicians it's time for a change.

Just the other day I was in Atlantic City with my family and an East Asian guy came up to me and said, "Thank you, Charlamagne, for speaking so loudly about the politicians. They drive me crazy the way they talk!" I don't know if this guy was a Republican, a Democrat, a vegan, or a Swiftie. I just know he was fed up.

Afterward my wife looked at me and said, "Yeah, it's starting to get a little crazy." What she meant was, I've had Black people coming up to me since *The Breakfast Club* first got big. A few white folks here and there. But something shifted once I started talking loudly about politicians. Folks I thought would never have a clue who I was were suddenly seeking me out. I'd struck a nerve.

Imagine if Kamala Harris was in a vice-presidential debate, and after her opponent made some outrageous claim, she simply sighed, shook her head, and said, "Wow, that is some bullshit."

Not "I'm afraid my opponent is misrepresenting the facts," or "It's extremely hypocritical for my opponent to say that given. . . ."

No, just "That is some bullshit!"

Sure some musty old commentators would write an op-ed about how inappropriate she had been. Fox would talk about her lack of dignity (cursing has got to be worse than a tan suit, right?).

But I believe most voters, particularly younger ones, would *love* it. They'd love that someone called out BS for what it was on a national stage. It would make them feel engaged. It would make them feel like a politician actually cared as much about the issues as they do themselves.

Because if you really care about the issues, how can you not call out BS for what it is? How can you not curse at least once? It seems impossible. It also seems inauthentic.

And while we're discussing ways that Republicans are more effective than the Democrats, another is the way they ride for their own.

I've noticed that when a Republican gets in some mess, or caught up in a scandal, they close ranks. They rally around the person instead of kicking them off the island.

Republicans will tolerate all sorts of shenanigans in their politicians. Corruption. Lies. Sharing secrets with foreign enemies. Hell, even staging a coup and trying to overthrow the government!

The thing they don't seem to tolerate is open homosexuality (the down low is fine though, of course). As I said one time on *The Daily Show*, the only corrupt politician I've ever seen the Republicans disown is George Santos. "Yes, he was a scam artist who stole and lied, but Republicans are ride and die with all kinds of liars and crooks," I told the crowd. "I'm just saying look at their track record. If you're LGBT they'll make you GTFO."

Republicans are very comfortable with corruption. From 1969 through 2020, Republican presidential administrations have had 121 criminal indictments and 89 convictions, while the Democrats have had 3 indictments and 1 conviction in the same period. And we're not even sure Trump has closed up his tab yet!

But you'll never hear the Republicans cop to any of that. They don't care if their politicians are pure. They care if they hold the party line.

I'd like to see a little more of that energy from the Democrats. I'm not saying I want them to start (openly) taking bribes, or start plotting ways to steal the White House. But they do need to start playing hardball more.

Democrats need to remember the public isn't demanding their politicians be "pure" anymore. We're demanding that they be effective.

To be clear, I'm not running for office. But I do pay way too much in taxes to keep my mouth shut. Especially when I have a platform I can reach people through.

We have to change how we talk about politics and how politicians talk to us. We can't do the same song and dance every four years and then wonder why things haven't improved, especially in the Black community.

Let's discuss. . . .

CHAPTER 8

Self-Destruction

Let's be honest—hip-hop has made a lot of Black folk rich. It's put a lot of us in positions to better their own circumstances and the circumstances of the people around them.

And even if they haven't personally made a dime off hip-hop, Black folks in general have benefited from hip-hop opening up white people's eyes to what's really going on with the African-American community. But, I often wonder, at what cost?

Hip-hop, at its heart, is a beautiful form of expression. It's right up there with jazz and rock 'n' roll as an American art form that has given a voice to the voiceless and changed how people view the world. Over the course of my lifetime, I can't think of a cultural force that's impacted not only America, but the world, more than hip-hop.

I know the elders who helped build that culture understood the power of hip-hop. Artists like KRS-One, Chuck D, and Queen Latifah truly used their platforms to educate and inspire. From systemic racism, to Pan-Africanism, spirituality, world history, and the cost of misogyny, these artists, and many others like them, used their voices to amplify meaningful topics.

But somewhere in the nineties and early 2000s those powerful messages started to get drowned out by a different kind of content: gangsta rap. Special Ed, the rapper behind classics like "I Got It Made" and

"The Mission," recently said that's not a specific enough time frame. He traces the start of this counterproductive small talk in hip-hop back to the late eighties, with the rise of N.W.A.

"N.W.A brought the age of destruction to hip-hop," he said on the *Drink Champs* podcast. "They brought the age of destruction to our children and culture. Period. . . . That's where it started. That's where the agenda and the destruction began."

Now, I can't fully cosign that statement because I was too young to know all of what was going on when N.W.A was poppin'. And I do know that through songs like "Fuck tha Police" the group, and especially Ice Cube, played a major role in bringing the harsh realities of life in places like South Central Los Angeles to the national stage.

It's pointless to try to identify individual people or points in time when this began, but I can wholeheartedly agree with Special Ed that hip-hop's "age of destruction" has worked to undermine its contributions elsewhere.

I know because I'm one of the people that was impacted by that destruction.

This is not meant to be an indictment of hip-hop. I can't blame hip-hop solely for my bad choices. My father worshipped James Brown (and hated most of the rappers who sampled him), but still made plenty of bad choices himself. Music alone cannot lead you down a path you would have not otherwise gone down.

But it can warp your understanding of what lies ahead for people who look and sound like you. It can make paths that in reality are filled with potholes and pitfalls seem well paved. It can make topics that deserve serious consideration seem inconsequential. In a world where we STILL struggle to find and elevate positive Black role models, musicians and entertainers are the most accessible examples of success available for a whole lot of young people. And when those entertainers are capitalizing on the exploitation of trauma (often exaggerated, if not completely fictional), things can go wrong.

My good brother, the writer and psychotherapist Resmaa Menakem, once wrote, "Trauma in a person, decontextualized over time, looks like personality. Trauma in a family decontextualized over time looks like family traits. Trauma in a people decontextualized over time looks like culture!"

Hip-hop started as a way to *transcend* our trauma. Its roots are in impoverished neighborhoods like the South Bronx where folks needed a way for the community to come together and have a good time—on the cheap. (Remember, the very first DJs plugged their turntables and speakers into streetlights. The first rappers performed in parks and playgrounds. These were people with very little in the way of resources.)

But over time that changed. It went from transcending trauma to contributing to it.

No need for me to sit here and single anyone out, but I'm also not going to act like hip-hop hasn't been profiting for a long time now off the trauma and dysfunction that exist in the ghetto. Whenever you have artists who didn't have these lived experiences rapping like they did just because it's what drives sales, that's when you know it's some bullshit (see how easy that was, Kamala?). The irony is that a lot of these artists start off pretending being street, but then actually end up *becoming* street because of the environment hip-hop creates around them.

As an elder in the hip-hop universe, I can say it's time to get honest and stop lying to ourselves about what some of these songs inspired so many of us to be and do. We are doing ourselves a disservice by not talking about that on a macro level, especially given that we live in an era that usually LOVES to dig up old shit and hold folks accountable for it. It's time for hip-hop to take some accountability.

I'm not calling for rappers to be canceled. I know rappers like Snoop Dogg, Nas, and Jay-Z have all put out much more thoughtful and nuanced material as they've matured.

What I'm calling for is for us, as a culture, to start amplifying the positive rappers coming up through the next generation of the game so that no one else feels forced to head down that path of trauma. Those voices are out there. I just worry they're not being heard as loudly as the voices that talk about pulling triggers, poppin' p***y, and getting money by any means necessary.

Hip-hop has so much sway over young people in this country and all around the world. What would our future look like if the most popular rappers were having big talks about issues like the environment, poverty, colonialism, technology, and yes, love. I'd feel so positive about our collective future.

The same way we negatively influenced people with *trauma* culture over the last thirty years, let's positively influence people with *healing* culture for the next thirty. I already see signs of it happening right now. I'm encouraged by Jay-Z with *4:44*, Kendrick Lamar with *Mr. Morale and the Big Steppers*, and Westside Boogie with *More Black Superheroes*.

I love hearing the next wave, people like LaRussell and Rapsody, process their emotional pain in music. Why? Because those are the conversations people, especially Black men, have historically run from. Not because we weren't impacted by that trauma, but because we were never taught or encouraged to be open about it. As a result, we turned to a lot of small talk about things that were supposed to make up for the damage we were feeling: who has the most money, who has the flyest car, who's killed the most people, who's sold the most drugs, and a whole bunch of other criminal shit that has done nothing but cause our communities pain.

That mentality hasn't done anything but lead to death and RICO charges. The "destruction" Special Ed spoke of.

Some call it the "hip-hop lifestyle," but I don't even like calling it that. It's a death style. And it's been a death style for a long time. That's why it's time to start talking and thinking BIG. If we refuse to recognize our flaws as a culture, how are we supposed to identify our strengths?

If we don't get honest, we are going to die lying and this "culture" we love called hip-hop is going to die with us.

Let's discuss. . . .

CHAPTER 9

Tree-Hug the Block

As a child, I spent a lot of time out in nature, exploring the dirt roads, streams, fields, and forests that dominate the landscape where I was raised in South Carolina.

From the time I was around eight years old till I finally got a Nintendo four or five years later, I spent every moment I could outdoors. Every single day felt like an adventure for my friends and me. Being outside was all we knew.

We'd meet at an appointed time and then just plot something to get into. "Let's ride our bikes to the BP gas station in Conifer Hall and get some Honey Buns," someone might say. Or maybe, "My daddy told me there are some old tombstones in the woods over by Old Whitesville Road."

And with that we'd be off, pedaling our bikes or just walking along the dirt roads. Often we'd get caught up in a new adventure along the way—"Hey, you see that diamondback rattlesnake under that rock? Don't go near it, they're poisonous!"

Whether we made it to our destination or not ultimately didn't matter. We just loved being outside under that low South Carolina sky. We didn't need amusement parks or playgrounds (or iPads and MacBooks) to entertain us. Mother Nature had us covered.

I learned a lot of things out in nature, and not just how to catch a snake or find your way through the woods without getting lost.

Nature is what taught me to embrace my imagination. When you're outside all day long until the sun sets, you're forced to explore. To take risks. To experiment. When you develop those abilities day after day, it can't help but translate to other aspects of your life. There's a reason so many writers and painters find inspiration in the outdoors. When you slow down and take in the majesty of nature, you start to notice miracles all around you. And then you want to create little miracles of your own.

Another thing I learned from nature was the power of slowing down. Remember, these were the days before cell phones. At the end of the day you might tell your friends, "OK, meet me tomorrow morning at 9:30 down by the big oak tree," but come the next morning, your friends were nowhere to be found.

If they had to clean up their rooms, or run an errand for their mother, there was no text message to tell you about the change in plans. It wasn't unusual to find yourself waiting an hour or more for people to show up. So you'd sit under that tree and watch the birds, feel the wind, and look at the sky. Nobody was staring at their phone or swiping through IG posts while they waited. No, they were soaking up nature.

It was the same with catching the bus. It might come in five minutes. Or in forty-five minutes. There was no app to tell you. So you'd wait. And wait. And the whole time you'd just take in the world around you. The sights, the smells, the sounds. Maybe you'd have a comic book to distract you for a few minutes, but ultimately you'd find yourself alone with your thoughts and Mother Nature.

Those moments helped create a sense of stillness in my life. A sense of ease.

When I look at some of the times when I've struggled with anxiety, I can see they were moments when I was missing that stillness.

And it was missing in large part because my connection from nature had been cut.

I have no doubt there's been a connection between my anxiety and spending less time outdoors. In fact, I recently saw a study led by Professor Gregory Bratman, then of Stanford University, that found a link between spending time in nature and reducing depression. According to the *Proceedings of the National Academy of Science,* people who walked for ninety minutes in a natural area, versus those who walked the same amount of time in an urban area, showed decreased activity in a part of the brain that is linked to a key factor in depression.[1]

"These results suggest that accessible natural areas may be vital for mental health in our rapidly urbanizing world," said Stanford professor Gretchen Daily, a coauthor of the study, to the Stanford News Service. Her findings also noted that people who live in cities have a 20 percent higher risk of anxiety disorders and a 40 percent higher risk of mood disorders than those who live in rural areas.

My own experiences back up that study's findings. When I was spending most of my time out in nature, I was happy. It's that simple. My anxiety didn't kick in until I was spending more and more time inside playing my Nintendo. Or watching *Rap City* on BET after school. Or hanging out in the McDonald's parking lot with my friends. The further I got from nature, the more my anxiety seemed to grow.

That's why when I recently bought a new house, I made sure it had plenty of land. We're currently sitting on four and a half acres. Nothing crazy by South Carolina standards, but pretty good for right outside New York City. Walk off my back porch and you're right in the woods.

That was at the top of my wish list when we were looking to buy a house. I didn't prioritize luxuries like wine cellars, home movie the-

- - - - - -

[1] Gregory N. Bratman et al., "Nature Experience Reduces Rumination and Subgenual Prefrontal Cortex Activation," *Proceedings of the National Academy of Sciences* 112, no. 28 (June 29, 2015): 8567–72, https://doi.org/10.1073/pnas.1510459112.

aters, or what kind of marble the kitchen countertop had. I wasn't worried about showing out for *MTV Cribs*. No, I prioritized *trees*.

It's so important to me that my kids have that access to nature. Sure, they spend time playing *Minecraft* and *Roblox* like their friends, but they also spend time in the woods. They might not realize it today, but those hours experiencing peacefulness in nature will have a deep impact on the rest of their lives.

I also try to set a good example for them with my own actions when it comes to spending time in nature. I'm on my phone too much and watching TV more than I'd care to admit, but I also make sure to carve out time every week to kick off my shoes and spend time just feeling the earth under my feet in our backyard.

I've become a big proponent of a practice called "grounding." It's also known as "earthing" and I've found it's one of the easiest ways you can improve your health—mental and physical—through nature. Here's how it works: kick off your shoes, find a safe piece of grass or dirt (no broken glass), and just walk around. Feel the earth underneath you and allow yourself to soak up all the healing energy it's giving you. Focus on your breath. I promise if you start your practice in an anxious state, you'll feel better in minutes.

According to the National Institutes of Health, a recent study on grounding has found that it also helps reduce inflammation, promotes better sleep, and improves blood flow.[2] I know so many folks who are struggling with their health that would benefit from this practice.

The other practice I use my backyard for is tree hugging. I know that when a lot of you hear the term "tree hugger," you probably think of

------

[2] James Oschman, Gaetan Chevalier, and Richard Brown, "The Effects of Grounding (Earthing) on Inflammation, the Immune Response, Wound Healing, and Prevention and Treatment of Chronic Inflammatory and Autoimmune Diseases," *Journal of Inflammation Research*, March 2015, 83–96, https://doi.org/10.2147/jir.s69656.

white hippies allergic to deodorant. That's fine. I used to think that way too. But let me tell you, today this proud Black man (who still loves deodorant) is a full-blown tree hugger.

Any chance I get, I walk out into my backyard, put my hands on a tree, lean my head against it, and start to meditate. That's tree hugging. It's a valuable practice I was taught by my sacred purpose coach, Yadi (more on her in a second). Here's how I first learned.

One day I was feeling between "O and K," which is my way of saying I wasn't falling apart, but I wasn't all the way together either. I was in a mood because I'd been thinking about my late friend the writer Jas Waters, aka Jas Fly.

You might already be familiar with some of Jas's work—she was a writer on the hit TV series *This Is Us*, as well as *The Breaks*. But more importantly, to the people who were close to her, Jas was someone you could really lean on for advice and inspiration. She was generous and compassionate. Jas would always check me when I needed checking and lift me up when I was down.

When she took her own life, it caught me by surprise. And really messed me up.

I wasn't sure how to process how I was feeling about Jas, so I called Yadi. Not surprisingly, Yadi knew just what I should do. "I want you to go outside and put your hands on one of the trees in your backyard," she told me. "Once you have your hand on it, lean your forehead against the tree and start to meditate."

Yadi's never guided me wrong, so I went outside, put my head against a big, beautiful tree in my backyard, and started taking deep, purposeful breaths. After a few minutes, the energy from that tree was radiating through my body and had put me in a better place. I immediately felt better.

Ever since then, I've been a literal, committed tree hugger. Just like with grounding, there is a strong belief that tree hugging has positive physical benefits. One theory is that when you hug a tree, it increases your levels of oxytocin. That's the hormone that helps promote calm and emotional balance. Tree hugging is also believed to release dopamine, which is going to make you feel happier.

We like to poke fun at tree huggers in America, but it's actually a respected practice around the world. In Japan, they call tree hugging *shinrin-yoku*, or "forest bathing." They believe it reduces stress levels, decreases blood pressure, and helps you heal from illness.

It's also valued in Iceland. During the pandemic, the forest service in Iceland actually went out and cleared paths to the forest so that people could get some quality tree hugging in.

I don't think there's anyone reading this book that couldn't benefit from a little tree time. Please, give it a try. It doesn't seem to matter what kind of tree you hug, though it does seem that the bigger the tree, the more energy you're going to get from it.

Pick your tree and then spread your arms as wide as you can around it. Then press your face against it. Spend a few minutes either meditating or just focusing on your breath.

If the idea of people seeing you pressed up against a tree makes you a little uncomfortable, then you can start by just sitting at the base of a tree with your back pressed against it. It won't look as crazy, but you'll still get some benefits.

Just how long do you have to hug a tree to get the desired effects? The general answer seems to be a minimum of five minutes. And it's recommended that you do it at least several times a week.

I especially recommend it for Black folks and other people of color. The stress we experience in America is on a different level. Every single one of us could use a practice that lowers our stress and blood pressure without involving pharmaceuticals. Just be mindful of where you do it. I don't want any headlines about how Charlamagne's book got someone arrested when a Karen called the cops on a young Black man hugging a tree in Central Park. I just know if they're OK calling the cops on Black birdwatchers, they'll damn sure call the cops on Black tree huggers too. Maybe try uptown or in Brooklyn first.

A quick word about Yadi. I've noticed often when I mention that I have a sacred purpose coach, people tend to laugh or even roll their eyes. That's cool. You might not be familiar with her title, but Yadi is an incredibly gifted and insightful person. If she'd done nothing else but introduce me to tree hugging, she would still have a tremendous influence on my life.

Recently I was discussing on *The Brilliant Idiots* how she taught me about tree hugging. "Yo, how much money do you spend a week on mental health shit?" Andrew asked me after I told him about Yadi. "A lot, baby," I responded. "Y'all go buy the Phantoms and the Ghosts, I'm investing in my mental health for real for real. I like therapy, my sacred purpose coach, my gemstones. All that shit."

Believe me, no matter how much money I earn, using it to support my—and my family's—mental health is going to be my priority. Before any material items, I'm going to spend on anything that brings me closer to priceless peace and serenity.

I've been very fortunate to be able to afford those resources. But I realize that not everyone can. What everyone can afford, though, is to spend more time in nature. Everyone can afford to walk around with their shoes off, no matter how silly that might make you feel. Even if you live in the Bronx or in Liberty City, there's a park *some-where* near you.

Get past whatever sort of perceptions the world has tricked you into believing about nature. No, you're not acting "white" or "goofy" by hugging a tree or walking around with your shoes off. You don't think our ancestors in Africa knew the value of feeling the dirt under their feet? Of course they did.

That's why when you practice grounding, you're honoring an ancient truth—that you can find peace and rejuvenation through nature. If anything, grounding and tree hugging should just be the start.

Let's discuss. . . .

CHAPTER 10

Astronaut Kids, Featuring Elliott Connie

Let's talk about how we talk with our kids.

And to do that, I want to have a conversation with someone I've truly come to admire, the psychotherapist Elliott Connie. He's a really brilliant African-American therapist who has truly expanded my understanding of mental health and how to build healthy relationships.

Recently one of our conversations turned to the best ways to inspire people, especially children. As the father of four daughters, it is something that is on my mind a lot. And I won't lie—despite all the time and money I spend making sure my own kids have access to the best, academically and culturally, I'm still anxious that I'm not doing enough.

So when I shared that fear with Elliott, he asked me, "Well, how did you answer the astronaut question?" I didn't understand what he was talking about, but once he explained, it made me appreciate the power of talking BIG to our kids. Like out-of-this-world BIG.

It was such a great conversation that I asked Elliott to share it with you all here:

What I mean by the astronaut question is this:

If a ten-year-old child approaches you and announces, "I wanna be an astronaut!," then the only question you can ask back is "Great, what planet do you want to visit?"

If you ask them any other question, such as, "Why do you think you could do that?" or "You ain't good at math, how you gonna be an astronaut?" then you are judging them in a negative way.

You might think you're motivating them by keeping them grounded to earth (no pun intended), but you're actually killing their ability to think someone believes in them. This is why if a ten-year-old comes up to me and says, "I wanna play professional basketball," then the only question I can ask them is "What team do you wanna play for?" Because any other question sounds like you don't believe in them. And I learned how important it is to listen with belief.

One of the things I noticed when I started learning about psychotherapy is that we study trauma, pain, symptoms, and medication. But we don't study hope. We don't study belief. And I think that's wrong. I think we're doing a real disservice to people who need hope and belief, especially children.

As therapists, teachers, and especially as parents, it's critical that we are sources of inspiration. That is so much more valuable than shielding a child from potential disappointment.

Because when a child tells you they want to be an astronaut, there are really only two possible outcomes. The first is they will achieve their aim and become an astronaut. The second outcome is they will learn something invaluable along the journey that makes the journey worthwhile even if they never actually make it into space.

I've seen this happen in my own life. If you had asked me what I wanted to be at ten years old, I would have shouted right back "A professional baseball player!" And that dream stayed with me for a long time. I went to college to play ball and figured it would help me get closer to the major leagues. Being a psychotherapist was the last thing on my mind.

But along the journey, I got a college degree, and that college degree has changed my life. For the better. I wasn't crushed that I didn't wind up a major-league baseball player. I was elated that I found a calling I had never anticipated for myself. One that's allowed me to touch people's lives in a meaningful way I would have never thought possible.

We have to stop trying to protect people from future disappointment and allow them to have dreams. That's because every single person, I don't care who it is, has a dream. So someone in their life has to believe in them. And if they don't have someone that believes in them, and you tell them something negative, it will crush them.

Just believe in them.

After Elliott told me that, I had to do some soul-searching. Because the truth is if I look back at my life, I have been more of a dream crusher than a dream supporter. Even as a kid, I can remember my mother saying, "You and your dad don't know how to talk to people." By that, she meant we were too direct. Too blunt. Too discouraging.

I can remember my father constantly telling me, "Boy, the fastest way between two points is a straight line." In other words, get straight to the point. Don't blow smoke up people's asses. Give them the hard truths they need to hear. If you went to my dad and said, "Hey, Big Larry, I want to start a BBQ in Moncks Corner, what do you think?" he'd give you all the reasons why it *wouldn't* work before saying, "Hey, but let's figure it out."

I carried a lot of that discouraging mentality out of my teenage years and into my career. As a radio DJ, doubting people almost became my calling card. I even used to bill myself as a "De-Motivational Speaker." It became such a part of my identity that I even labeled a chapter in my first book, *Black Privilege*, "Fuck Your Dreams."

I put my belief into practice. As my stature grew in the entertainment field, people would constantly ask me for career advice. If I thought they sounded wack as a rapper, I'd say, "Fuck your rap dreams. You suck." If they wanted to be on the radio and I didn't think they had what it takes, I'd say, "Fuck your radio dreams." I thought I was doing those people a favor. I even used to say, "If you don't have anything nice to say . . . say it anyway."

I maintain my motives weren't bad—I was really trying to save people from disappointment and wasting their time—but as Elliott taught me, it wasn't my job to protect people from failing. My job—and the job of all of us—is to encourage people to reach as high as they can.

After talking with Elliott, I had to do a lot of soul-searching. After reflecting, I decided I had leaned into my "De-Motivational Speaker" character too hard.

Having children of my own also made me reassess how I was using my words. What's crazy is that one of my daughters literally wants to be an astronaut. She's imagined a whole planet that's named after her. Everything revolves around space for her. We've taken her on trips to the Air and Space Museum in Washington, DC, and the Liberty Science Center, which is near us in New Jersey. My wife and I don't discourage her obsession with space—we provide every resource available to help her realize her dreams.

My daughter and her sisters are also passionate about writing. Poetry, fiction, plays—you name it. One of her favorite things to do is stage plays with her sisters. Each of the kids gets a role and she scripts the whole thing out. Then she'll insist my wife and I sit and watch the entire performance.

My daughter knows I own Black Privilege Publishing (the publisher of this very book) and she's even asked me, "Dad, are you going to publish my book?"

Now, when she said that, I didn't say, "Honey, it's really hard to get published. Even if your daddy runs the company. There's just a lot of competition out there. It might be smarter to focus on something else."

Instead, I said, "Damn right I'm going to publish it." And even if I didn't have my own imprint, I still would have encouraged her to work her ass off writing. And when the time was right, I would have worked my ass off to find a publisher for her.

All my kids are extremely comfortable with their dreams. Extremely comfortable with their place in this world.

I'll never forget when I got invited to the premiere of Ava DuVernay's *A Wrinkle in Time*. Before the film started, all the celebrities were hanging out and *the* Oprah Winfrey actually came over to where we were standing. This was my first time meeting Oprah, so I definitely had a sense of excitement.

But not my daughter. She looked up at Oprah and nonchalantly said, "Oh yeah, I did a book report on you once." Oprah was incredibly gracious and asked her about the report, but even then my daughter wasn't impressed. She was hardly engaged in the conversation. I actually got upset. I wanted to pull her aside and hiss in her ear, "Listen, you are talking to *royalty*. Show some respect."

But in retrospect, why should I expect my daughter to react to a situation the way I would have as a kid? We grew up in completely different environments, with completely different experiences. I've worked hard to give her the confidence and exposure to culture that makes meeting Oprah Winfrey feel manageable.

Again, I grew up poor, in a single-wide trailer. My family constantly had to worry about money. That's never been a concern for my kids. My kids have access to everything. Even the queen herself!

Still, I sometimes I get anxious about my kids' situation. I find myself wanting to inject a little struggle into their lives. I tell myself that it's to "toughen them up," but don't ask me to explain why because . . . I can't.

The goal is to raise happy, trauma-free children. There's no value in injecting artificial struggle into their experience.

Just as there's no value in me injecting struggle or any form of negativity into anyone else's experience. This is why I've become very intentional in changing my whole approach in how I talk not only to my kids, but to everyone.

The "De-Motivational Speaker" who was injecting small, negative talk into people's lives every day is gone. There's no positive reason to undermine an aspiration. I'm fully committed to evolving into someone who only gives big encouragement and big support when someone comes to me with their dreams.

Let's discuss. . . .

CHAPTER 11

Funny or Die

I don't care how serious the situation is, I'm going to crack a joke.

That doesn't mean I don't take the situation seriously. Just the opposite, in fact.

I've learned that if you really want to engage people in big, meaningful talk, then injecting humor into the conversation is a great way to do it.

Everyone thinks clearer—and more expansively—when information is delivered with laughter. It's the same level of focus you acquire with post-nut clarity.

Which is why we're living in a very critical moment right now. To put it plainly, people have become too damn sensitive to all sorts of subjects: politics, sexuality, race, gender—the list goes on and on. Topics that used to be the fuel for comedians' stand-up sets, shows like *Saturday Night Live*, or even just conversations with friends are now off-limits.

Call it "cancel culture." Call it "woke-ism." Call it "political correctness." Whatever you call it, I think we need to really consider how it's impacting our ability to navigate difficult subjects.

Before I go any further on this topic, I want to address what some of you might be thinking right now: Charlamagne is the *last* person that should be talking about the dangers of cancel culture.

And the irony is that there are two distinctly different groups of people thinking that, each coming from wildly different perspectives.

The first group thinks I shouldn't be talking about the danger of cancel culture because I should have *already canceled* myself. They don't like the way I've interacted with some of my guests on the radio over the years (and as I'll explain later, I don't necessarily disagree with them) and want me silenced.

Then there's another group that used to love my old antics and thinks I've gone soft. To them, I've become "PC Tha God," a play on my moniker "C Tha God." The way they see it, I've already become a leader in the woke mob.

I would like to tell both these groups to suck my dick.

Respectfully.

But no matter what people think of me, or how I might or might not have changed over the years, what hasn't changed is that I love to engage with the world through humor.

Humor was a major part of my life growing up. And not just any kind of jokes either—I'm talking dark humor. Things were rough where I'm from, and the best—and cheapest—tool folks had to deal with their conditions was jokes. And believe me, nothing was off-limits. My father and my cousin Rel were determined to get their jokes off, no matter what the circumstances.

The newspaper that covered Moncks Corner was called the *Berkeley Independent*. And like any small-town newspaper, everything made its pages. The taxman coming to take away someone's trailer? The *Independent* was going to cover it. Someone got their car repossessed? Or lost a relative to drugs? All of that was going to wind up in the *Independent*.

As soon as new issues would come out, my father and Rel would be skimming through the pages looking for situations—usually messed-up ones—that they could joke about. It was some of the darkest humor I'd ever heard.

They still joke like that to this day. Recently quite a few people in Moncks Corner that my father knew have passed away. It felt like there was a funeral every day.

To my father, who made a point to always fry fish for the family of the deceased, it was a situation that could only be addressed with a joke. "Man, I can't stand it when all these folks die at the same time," he told me. "You know how much fish I gotta fry now? The shit ain't cheap! They need to space these deaths out!"

It was ruthless humor, but it also offered a way to cope. In a town where folks were always getting in some shit—having their cars repossessed, getting hauled off to jail, or dying way too young—jokes were the best way to make sense of it all. To confront what had happened and then start the healing process. I can't lie, sometimes the jokes were just attempts to get a laugh—no matter how inappropriate they were. One of my father's favorite bits back in the day when he was working the bar at his spot was to make fun of any man who ordered something sweet to drink. Order a Smirnoff Ice or Mike's Hard Lemonade and my father would yell at the top of his lungs, "Get him an ice cold f****t, please." Sometimes he would even ask, "Would you like your f****t neat or on the rocks?" Terrible, I know. But unfortunately this is what passed for acceptable humor in a small Southern town during the era when Eddie Murphy's *Raw* was king.

Not that anyone explained any of this context to me. At the time, I just knew nothing was off-limits, and if you wanted to survive, joking was how to do it.

It's an approach that I've carried with me through life. Anything that makes me uncomfortable, I try to make a joke out of it. That's why I'm so self-deprecating.

Take, for example, my well-documented insecurity about the size of my penis. It went back to college, when my now wife and I were dating. We had broken up for a stretch, and when I tried to convince her to get back together with me, she somehow let it slip that one of the guys she had been with during our break was definitely packing more of a punch than I was.

Now, that's a special kind of pain that's pretty tough for a guy to recover from. Still, I knew the only way to start the healing process was to put the information out there and let the jokes start flying— at my expense.

I've gotta be the only hip-hop media personality who's ever spoken about the size of his penis, and yes it was small talk. Who has openly admitted to taking those pills they used to sell in the back of *XXL* magazine (Magna RX). Who has told millions of people that he tried doing those penis exercises where you keep pulling on the tip to stretch it out and make it bigger (hey, maybe it worked, because we're married now).

Now contrast my approach with the actions of Mr. Kanye West after he found out his wife slept with Pete Davidson, who possesses true BDE (you know what that stands for).

After he found out about Pete and Kim, Kanye literally called me and begged me to help him ruin Pete's reputation. I tried to explain to Kanye that not only was Pete my friend, but he hadn't done anything wrong. Kanye wasn't trying to hear it. "My wife is out here f--king a white boy with a ten-inch penis, and you won't help me?" he yelled at me. "You're telling me that's your friend, but you're supposed to be culture?"

Now, obviously *that* was a hysterical reaction. The problem was Kanye wasn't trying to be funny. He was dead serious.

If Kanye had just been able to joke about not being able to, ahem, measure up with a white boy, it would have helped him heal from that trauma much easier. In fact, if you look at the women Kanye's dated since breaking up with Kim, it's pretty clear he *still* hasn't gotten over her.

Speaking of Pete, he's another person who has used humor to deal with his trauma. In Pete's case, it's how he's dealt with the death of his father, Scott Matthew Davidson, a firefighter who died in the Twin Towers on 9/11. Pete's constantly making jokes about his father and how he passed. He even named one of his comedy special's *SMD*, which is not only the initials for one of the acts keeping Kanye up at night, but is also his father's initials.

Healing through humor.

I know I've volunteered way too much information—it's a little scary that my penis size is out there like that. I'm sure it's embarrassing for my wife and family. I won't lie, it makes me cringe just thinking about it.

Humor plays a huge role in politics too.

Do you know why Donald Trump is one of the most dangerous humans to ever walk the face of the earth? Because he's so funny.

He talks funny, his stance is funny, his hair is hilarious . . . everything about him screams humor. And when he goes at his opponents, I can't lie, he's got jokes. If he were still just the host of *The Apprentice*, or making cameos in movies, you'd be able to just laugh at him.

Unfortunately, some people like him largely because he's so funny. His humor camouflages most of the awful things he's done and terrible ideas he's had.

Millions of people don't see the awful stuff because he's funny. It's why young rappers like Sexyy Red and Kodak Black like him (in Kodak's case getting a pardon from him didn't hurt either). They think Trump is entertaining. The same qualities that made him a good TV host.

You simply cannot lose with humor (though in Trump's case, I hope he does).

My belief in the power of humor, especially when it comes to shaping people's political opinions, is why I'm so happy to appear from time to time on the institution that is *The Daily Show*.

Every time I'm guest hosting or appearing on the show, I spend time talking to the show's incredible showrunner, Jen Flanz, and her staff about its history. It was created back in 1996 with Craig Kilborn, and in 1999 Jon Stewart took over as host for what most know it to be today—real political satire. He wanted to help give that kind of content a platform on television. Jon understood that the most effective way to address real issues was through the lens of humor.

While I love that *The Daily Show* is still running strong all these years later, I am worried that people don't seem to respect the art of satire as much anymore. Satirical shows like my friend Aaron McGruder's *The Boondocks*, or my other friend Stephen Colbert's *The Colbert Report*, really demonstrate how it is possible to talk about important issues in ways that are entertaining and accessible.

I don't see that many shows like that around anymore. Which is why protecting platforms like *The Daily Show* is so important. There's something about the type of humor it uses that transcends race and class.

One night I went out to dinner with my wife during a week I was hosting *The Daily Show*. We went to an Italian restaurant not far from my house, one that we've been to plenty of times before. No one's ever recognized me, or approached me in any way.

But this time a bunch of white people—older ones especially—stopped by our table to say hello. They'd all seen *The Daily Show* and said they'd been impressed. "I watched you on *The Daily Show*," one much older white guy told me. "I like the way you hold these politicians accountable. Don't let up on them!"

"I appreciate that, my brother," I told him. "And I promise you I won't!"

I'm going to keep my promise to that old white man too. I'm going to stay on these politicians, but I'm going to use humor to do it because laughter is truly the best medicine, unless you're uncontrollably laughing for no reason and don't seem to know why. In that case you probably need some medicine, some therapy too, fuck it just put the straitjacket on and enter the padded room.

Let's discuss. . . .

CHAPTER 12

The Lying Game

My father always told me, "You're not lying to me, you're lying to yourself." It took me a long time to understand the depth of those words, but now I comprehend them fully.

We lie to ourselves and then volunteer the lies we tell ourselves to other people.

It's a terrible trait.

Lying to yourself is bad enough, but volunteering that same lie to other folks in your life should have you committed. I've done it, we all have done it.

The biggest lies we tell ourselves are excuses. The little fairy tales we make up in our minds to justify some of the foul moves that we've made. The treacheries we perform and backstabbing we engage in that we'd rather not admit to. That makes us so uncomfortable about ourselves that instead of facing our failings head-on, we create fictional scenarios to make us feel better about ourselves. Of course those scenarios have just enough truth weaved into the fantasy that we can almost convince ourselves that they're real. But none of our excuses are made out of 100 percent pure silk or wool. They've all got way more polyester in them than we want to admit.

One of our favorite fairy tales to create—and I'm guilty of doing this myself—is the one where we are the hero and someone else is the villain.

You know, the scenario where you take credit for someone's work, or let down a friend, or are slow to pay back a loan, or betray someone's trust, but somehow try to act like you were forced into that position. The scenario where as the hero, you only made that hurtful choice because you were left with no other choice. And then not only do we weave that fantasy in our minds, but we go even further and share it with our friends. We present it in a way that makes our friends likely to respond with, "No, you weren't the bad guy, I understand why you did what you did." It's a foul thing to do on two levels. Not only have you let down the actual victim in the story, but you've compounded that damage by making folks feel the victim somehow deserved their treatment.

I've done this in the past. Especially in regards to women, being the friend that a man trusts around his lady, only to end up sleeping with his "friend's" girl. I was clearly the bad guy, but I lied to myself and said, "No, the woman is actually the bad one here because she initiated it!" As if I didn't have a say in the matter.

Being that foul leaves a sickening feeling in your gut, but especially when you get confronted about it and double down on that LIE. It's much healthier to admit that you were the villain in the situation from the start. Admit that you betrayed someone and feel terrible about it. Confess that you are digusted by your actions and you want to make it right. You can create something positive out of those feelings. But don't hold on to the lie you told yourself. Especially when it involves a scenario that happened when you were younger and were still very much a work in progress. Give yourself some grace and realize that just because you did something stupid when you were coming up doesn't mean you have to carry that lie with you for the rest of your life.

No matter what sort of stupid shit you might have done in the past, there is absolutely a point in life where GOD gives you choices to make in regards to whatever generational trauma you are repeating. You have to make a conscious decision at that moment to either break the cycle or continue the lie. If you choose to continue the lie, well trust me when I tell you that's not going to end well. In the words of Pops from *Friday*, "That's your ass, Mr. Postman."

God has granted me a lot of moments to break the cycle, but there's no question the most significant have been via my relationship with my wife.

I've already spoken on how re-committing to my relationship with my wife was the single best thing I've ever done in my life, but I want to address how I found the courage to make that commitment: it has been through the example of my wife herself. Because even as I continued to screw up, my wife never wavered in showing me what a perfect spouse and best friend looked like.

My wife has a lot of admirable qualities, but one of her greatest is that she never wavers.

Once my wife fucks with you, she fucks with you forever. She might not let people in very easily, but when you pass that test, you're good with her forever. When it comes to family and friends, she's going to be the one who shows up every time. When someone is going through a rough period, my wife is going to be the one they know they can always call. My wife doesn't ghost people. Doesn't say she'll call them right back and then disappear. Promise help one day and act like she never did the next. Nope. My wife is someone you can always count on.

So even when I was lying to myself about my own loyalty, about my own character, in my wife I could see the standard I needed to measure up to. She showed me what it looked like to stand strong even though the winds of dysfunction and toxicity are blowing at a hurricane speed all around you. The strength of my wife's truth made my little fantasies so sad by comparison that I finally had to face them head-on.

While we're speaking on my wife, it should be said that the other principle she won't compromise on is honesty. Hell, she probably should have written this book instead of me!

My wife doesn't lie. Not about money, or friends, or how she's feeling. She won't even tell little white lies just to make folks feel better. Nope. If I ask my wife, "How does my outfit look?," she won't just glance in my direction and say, "Great," before getting back to her show. If I look busted, she'll say so. If she thinks one of my interviews was bad, she'll tell me. My wife does not bullshit, ever. I don't think she's every BS'd anyone in her life.

Some people are afraid to partner with someone like that, but it's been a lifesaver for me. I have major trust issues, so being with someone who doesn't lie gives me a lot of security. She's really the perfect counterbalance to me.

It seems like it's been that way forever. Forget about shooting in the gym. To take Drake's analogy and apply it to my wife and I, she wasn't just in the gym with me. She's been shootin' with me on Nerf courts hanging from my bedroom door! Meaning, she has been on every single step of this journey with me. Literally the first time I ever went to a radio station to fill out an application for an internship, my wife drove me because my license was suspended. I'm on this path because she put me on it.

Yes, I have trust issues. But one thing I don't have is a prenup. If I were married to any other woman in the world, I'd have a prenup longer than Victor Wembanyama's arms. But I wouldn't even dream of asking my wife to sign one. How stupid would I look asking this angel whose held me down for over twenty years to sign a piece of paper detailing what she "deserves." She deserves it all. Because she's earned it all. Including my love and commitment.

Now, at the end of every episode of *The Brilliant Idiots*, there's a segment called "Ask an Idiot." As the title suggests, it's a chance for listeners to ask an idiot (in this case Andrew Schulz or myself) any questions they might have.

One week I received the following question from a listener named Julie165.

"Charlamagne, what is the one thing you love about your wife?" she asked.

Now, that's a question I'm always happy to answer. But on that particular day, I was *really* ready to answer it. That's because my wife and I had just come back from a spiritual retreat together where it had really been made clear to me just what a special woman she is and how important she has always been to me.

But that weekend also made me think about some of the fake fantasies I'd tried to tell her over the years, the times where I'd tried to tell her that I was the hero when I was really the villain. The moments that make me very ashamed when I think back on them.

So I decided to really open up not only to Julie165, but the world.

"I have a million things I love about my wife," I said. "A million, million, things. But I love my wife for who she is. And has always been that."

Even though we'd been together since we were teenagers, I went on to explain, she's never changed. I'm like a roller coaster. I'm up, I'm down. I'm back up again. Being in a relationship with me can be wild.

My wife, on the other hand, is steady. Stoic. Stable.

She's human, of course. She has her ups and downs too (a lot of them triggered by me).

But her incredible gift is that she never loses sight of who she is and what her core principles are.

I just wish I had always been truthful with myself about how important she is to me. We met as kids, and I carried a lot of that young behavior with me for too long.

Thankfully, she's blessed me with the space to get myself together. We started off as kids and now we've got our own kids. And I can't wait to be a grandparent with her, playing with our kids' kids. There's nobody on this earth I'd rather do life with than her and I'm glad I stopped lying to myself about that.

Let's discuss. . . .

CHAPTER 13

World Wide Nigga Net

Niggas. Niggas. Niggas. Niggas. Niggas.

Why did I write that word five times?

That's easy. To get it out of my system.

That's because I'm done with niggas.

I used to always say I don't talk to niggas after 5 p.m. At this point in my life I don't want to talk to niggas at any time on the clock.

OK, I'll start using "N-word" now because some of you are probably getting pretty uncomfortable (and some of you white-bodied niggas is probably getting too comfortable).

And the particular type of N-words that I want to get out of my system are the ones I encounter every day on social media.

You've probably heard of "Black Twitter," right? Well, that's not what I'm talking about. I want to speak on what I call the WWNN, or World Wide Nigga Net.

What's the difference? Well, on Black Twitter there are quality conversations, insightful information, and laugh-out-loud funny jokes. Black Twitter features creatives and intellectuals doing what they do best: taking a platform or space that wasn't built for them, but making it their own. Breathing life, love, energy, and innovation into something and pushing it to its highest version of itself.

The WWNN, however, is another story. You won't find creativity, insightfulness, and inspiration on the WWNN. All you'll find is low vibrations.

Those low vibrations are coming from everywhere. The manosphere, political fanatics, conspiracy theorists, people who post fight videos, not to mention bored people who will constantly dig up old tweets just to start a fire on your name via social media. The people who love to spread misinformation because all they want is engagement on the WWNN.

One of the great dangers of the WWNN is that it leads to people viewing *all* their content through the same lens. Folks apply the same amount of critical analysis (or lack thereof) to Katt Williams speaking from the couch on *Club Shay Shay* as President Biden speaking from the Oval Office. In their minds, there's no difference between a streamer like Kai Cenat and Donald Trump. Everything, and everybody, is a form of entertainment. Even when extremely serious issues are at stake.

Speaking of Trump, when I use the "N-word," that's just a term I use to represent nonsense. It certainly doesn't only apply to Black folks. In fact, I love calling white people N-words. Or more specifically, I like to call them vanilla-flavored N-words. Donald Trump? Absolutely a vanilla (OK, orange) N-word. Marjorie Taylor Greene? One of the biggest vanilla N-words alive. In fact, I wish someone would walk up to her and say, "You white supremacist NIGGA." Her head would probably explode. Nothing would upset her more than being called a slur historically reserved for African-Americans.

The point is, this isn't about putting the value of white content over Black content. Or trying to cross over from Black conversations to the mainstream. This is about valuing content that uplifts, instead of dragging you down.

Back in 1990, KRS-One released an album called *Edutainment*, where he very successfully synthesized Afrocentricity and political consciousness with entertainment. It was a great idea, and songs like "Love's Gonna Get'cha (Material Love)," "Beef," and "Original Lyrics" conveyed very deep concepts in accessible ways. The album was a truly successful blend of education and entertainment.

Unfortunately, KRS-One's form of edutainment never caught on the way it should have. So thirty-five years later, we're stuck with a new version of edutainment via the WWNN. One where mindlessness is held in the highest esteem while real education and enlightenment are tossed in the garbage.

The problem is once you're captured by the WWNN, it's very hard to get out of it. Why? Because it's fueled by algorithms that are just going to keep feeding you more and more low-vibrational content. Soon you'll start to believe that everyone is seeing the world through the same lens as you. But they aren't. They are (at least some of them, we pray) conversing on a much higher plane in their feed while you're yapping away on the WWNN. It's interesting to me how we have always used the phrase "surfing the web," because that's literally what so many people choose to do nowadays. Those of y'all riding those low-vibrational waves until they wipe you out (or even drown you).

And especially damaging about the negative algorithm is how few of us care to recognize that it's a problem at all. We know what too much alcohol does to a person over time. That's why we have AA, or Alcoholics Anonymous. Well, a lot of you out there need a new "AA"—Algorithm Anonymous. Because you're addicted to these algorithms just as bad as some folks are to Hennessy. And just like too much booze, they're both poisoning you from the inside out.

To be fair, there are voices out there asking real questions and sparking real conversations. I think Amanda Seales is a great example of this. Amanda has made a choice to use her voice, first earned through comedy, writing, and entertainment, in a productive way about issues like racism, sexism, and our country's appetite for war, that might ultimately be to the detriment to her career. I'm sure she has already lost people in Hollywood due to some of her positions. But she's committed to having conversations about topics that matter, no matter where you land on them, or whatever their cost.

But Amanda shouldn't be an outlier. There are so many issues that should be motivating people to stop focusing on being entertained and start focusing on the issues. *Roe v. Wade* being overturned should have had people putting down their phones and heading into the streets. Affirmative action being taken away in college should have the campus overrun with protests. What Republicans want to do to the Voting Rights Act should have people marching right now. The attempted coup by our former president should have people protesting every day. I could go on and on.

But I don't feel like people think these situations are real. It's almost like they think they're just another development on their favorite reality show or plot twist on their favorite drama. But these situations are all too real, and when these chickens finally come home to roost, there's not going to be anybody around to eat them because we as a society will be the ones to be collectively fried.

Now I can hear some of you saying, "Char, aren't you contributing to those conversations on the World Wide Nigga Net through *The Breakfast Club*?" I get it. It's a legitimate question.

The nature of shows like *The Breakfast Club* has been to engage in some of that small talk.

And I've certainly provided my share of low-vibrational content over the years. But what I've been focused on recently, and will remain focused on moving forward, is engaging in these entertaining stories, but finding a way to also make them educational. So yes, I will get on *The Breakfast Club* and talk about Katt Williams's interview with Shannon Sharpe, but I will try to do it in a way that finds the larger lesson in a conversation like that.

When I discussed that interview, where Katt aired out all his frustrations with the entertainment industry and other comedians who he felt had wronged him in the past, I took care to say that while it's fine to be entertained by Katt, please do not think that what worked for him will also work for you. Meaning, Katt can talk about a lot of different folks because he's put in the work for years and has a tremendous amount of credibility, both within the entertainment industry and outside of it.

If you're a young comedian, podcaster, or even just working an everyday job to put food on the table and deciding you're going to raise your profile at work by talkin' trash about everyone you've ever met, regardless of if it's true or not true, then trust me when I tell you it's not going to work. In fact, it's going to backfire. Doors will be shut to you that you didn't even know existed. You know how in the movies they have those bookcases that when you pull out the right book, suddenly a secret door opens? Well, that's what the workplace is like for everybody, quiet as it's kept. It's filled with hidden doors. So if you're talking shit and making enemies, you won't even know that door is there. It'll just never be open for you.

And believe me, I know that is what Katt was talking about! Gatekeepers not letting us in!! Well would *you* open the door of your establishment to somebody that was talking shit about you? That's just not how life works! Nobody is going to do a favor for the person who thinks they can pop off about whatever they want *about anybody* they want, and expect to be welcomed with open arms. I hope people don't learn the wrong lessons from that *Club Shay Shay* interview, because Katt Williams is a one-man operation who can fill an arena in any city in America. That's a very specific lens to experience the world through, but in the WWNN era I've already seen people acting like they need to take the Katt approach to their white-collar and blue-collar jobs. But I promise that the Katt approach will get you fired.

It's not just the entertainment industry, it's all industries. A lot of the doors that lead to success are hidden. They're not obvious. Sure, a lot of companies advertise positions or post jobs online. But the doors to many good jobs are opened through word of mouth and relationships. That's true from interns to CEOs. You're not going to get walked through those doors if someone goes online and sees you acting a damn fool. Your social media is a behavioral history that bosses will check.

I'm talking about stunts in Walmart, that dumb shit where folks were opening up items, licking them, and putting them back, or the other foolish prank where people were walking up behind folks in grocery stores and kissing them on the back of the neck, or making threats out loud, then when confronted they acted like they were on the phone. Not only will that keep you from getting a meaningful job, it also may get you locked up or shot! Yes, you might get some "likes" online. You might get your video shared, you might get all the engagement your heart desires. But you'll also potentially keep doors shut that you might have been able to walk through at some point.

Trust me, I've engaged in this sort of foolishness myself. Looking back, I can see how much pain I projected onto others for the sake of entertainment.

When I see folks who are willing to say anything and attack anyone for attention, I shake my head, because I remember that feeling. I know that behavior is eating them alive on the inside. (Well, some of them are just sociopaths so maybe not, but for me a lot of the things I was doing and saying were driving me crazy.)

Over the years I saw how the things I'd said had unintended consequences for me and unintended consequences for the people I said those things about. Total BS that I thought I needed to do as a guy on the come up, seeking attention and approval from anyone who would give it. I couldn't differentiate between good attention and bad attention. I was caught up in the same game you see these people degrading themselves to get TikTok numbers today.

It's precisely because I've engaged in this sort of behavior that you should listen to me. I can tell you from experience that in addition to the people I've hurt, I've lost plenty of opportunities because of my past bullshit. That's why I'm committed to using platforms like this book, or *The Breakfast Club*, to foster larger conversations and share what I've learned—simply because when you know better, then you do better.

If you look at who we've talked to on *The Breakfast Club* over the last eight years, you can see we're doing better. Joe Biden, Hillary Clinton, Bernie Sanders, Kamala Harris, Elizabeth Warren, Cory Booker, Larry Elders, Vivek Ramaswamy, Nikki Haley, Tim Scott, Bakari Sellers, Tim Ryan, President Barack Obama . . . man, the list goes on and on. Some of those interviews made headlines, others didn't get a ton of views. But I'm not worried about ratings, or whether I "won" a debate with a candidate. I'm just happy I'm exposing my audience to some of the people who are going to be deciding what the future of this country looks like.

The idea of *only* contributing to the WWNN makes me sick. Just like it makes a lot of other folks in positions like mine sick too. The difference is they just don't want to admit it. Trust me, a lot of your favorite hosts and podcasters don't want to be part of this WWNN nonsense anymore. They just have no idea on how to pivot. They're afraid that if they evolve, their audience won't want to evolve with them.

Not me. I'm going to embrace anything that allows me to have meaningful conversations. That's why I love appearing on *The Daily Show* from time to time. *The Daily Show* is my antidote to the WWNN. And no, not because it's a "white" show. First of all, it isn't. Trevor Noah was the host for almost ten years and helped foster some truly enlightening conversations about race and society. Just as Jon Stewart did before him and will surely do again.

I love *The Daily Show* because it allows us to have serious conversations in an accessible and entertaining way. I felt like I could use that platform to literally warn America of what's about to happen, but deliver that message in a way that people can understand and also find funny.

I know my old homies back on the WWNN don't like it. "Oh, Charlamagne's leaning into politics so he can be down with white people," they'll say. Or "He must have been bought off by the Democrats" (or Republicans, depending on who you ask). But none of that is true. Politics is one of many things, including mental health and mindfulness, that I'm leaning into because I'm a forty-five-year-old man who doesn't only want to be talking about the same things he talked about at twenty-five. We all need to understand that there's a whole other world out there that the WWNN isn't discussing, and it's a world that's going to shape our future whether we choose to take part in the planning of that future or not.

Let's discuss. . . .

CHAPTER 14

Listen to the Elders, Bro

We've segregated ourselves by generations. Boomers talking to Boomers. Gen X to Gen X. Millennials to Millennials. Gen Z to Gen Z.

It's time to get back to talking across generations.

You see so much of it online with language and memes specific to each age group, sometimes it feels like Americans of different generations are literally communicating in different languages from each other.

You can see this generational segregation in person too. Go to a pub, or a market, in other countries and you'll see people from different generations interacting with each other. Talking, laughing, dancing.

Here, you don't see sixty-year-olds hanging out in hookah joints (and if you did, you'd label them "old men in the clubs"). You don't often see twenty-year-olds hanging out in the same bars where fifty-year-olds like to go. The closest you might come to that sort of generational mixing is adults brawling with each other at their kids' birthday parties at Chuck E. Cheese.

But by shutting ourselves off from other generations, especially our elders, we're losing access to so much wisdom.

It hasn't always been this way. Growing up, I used to gravitate to adults. I was that kid always looking to hang around my dad, my uncles, and my grandma. I knew they had life experience to share with me and I wanted to soak up as much as possible.

My peers only seemed to have bad ideas to share. They wanted to push me toward trouble. Guns, police, speeding cars with drunk drivers. My elders wanted to steer me away from those things. They made me feel safe.

Even still, as I grew older myself, I often lost sight of what my elders were trying to share with me. I was particularly stupid during my mid-twenties, when I was on air in Columbia, South Carolina. Somehow it got into my head that the older DJs and radio folk were trying to hold me back.

So I made a mixtape called *Disrespect Your Elders*, which was basically just what it sounded like: me making fun of anyone on my station and in the industry that was older than me. I even started a crew with my boy DJ Frosty called The Future. All our energy was focused on getting rid of the "old guard" and putting ourselves in charge.

Today I cringe thinking about our "movement." Looking back, no one was holding me back or shutting me out. I was just jealous of what other people had accomplished and lacked the confidence that I would be able to pull off something similar on my own. I overcompensated for that insecurity by attacking those who had come before me. And wasted a lot of energy and time in the process.

Today, I celebrate those that paved the road I'm currently walking. I do everything I can to cultivate relationships with those pioneers. I'm very proud to say that I can reach out to people like Steve Harvey, Tyler Perry, Jay-Z, Robert Smith, Minister Farrakhan, Bishop T. D. Jakes, Arsenio Hall, and Bob Pittman for advice and inspiration. These living legends will not only reach back when I reach out, but they actually pour their knowledge into me. Just like my dad and grandma used to do back in the day.

One of the greatest experiences I've ever had was sitting down with the late, great music executive Clarence Avant, aka "the Black Godfather." He was around ninety years old at the time, but he still made time to break bread with me and talk for hours. Like me, Clarence was from the Carolinas (in his case North) but unlike me, he came up during the forties, a period when it was even more difficult for a Black man from the South to make it in the entertainment industry. Nevertheless, Clarence fought his way to Los Angeles, where he started several important record labels, as well as founded the first African-American-owned radio station in the city's history. For decades, Clarence was *the* guy in LA, the person you could talk to when you needed to make something happen or wanted to make a connection that seemed just out of reach.

And do you know what Clarence brought with him when he sat down with me?

A folder full of information.

He'd brought letters from former presidents and other memorabilia that he wanted to share with me. Clarence Avant was a guy who had already carved out his legacy and was still hungry to share bits of insights with me. He also wanted to know about the current state of terrestrial radio, about podcasts, about how social media impacted my job. He was as interested in learning from me as I was from him.

And I've noticed that Clarence isn't the only legend who still has that approach.

If there's a common thread that runs between all those successful people I've just mentioned, it's this: *a desire to teach combined with a desire to keep learning.*

Steve Harvey doesn't need to learn anything new. Neither does Jay-Z. Or Tyler Perry. They're all set for the rest of their lives and their children's lives too. But they're not satisfied with the success they've had. They want to keep building. To keep educating themselves. To stay up on whatever is happening now, instead of living in the past.

One time I reached out to Hov when he first launched Tidal and told him he should put podcasts on the platform. His response was

"Cool, but you need to school me on the podcast thing." Of course I was more than happy to even share whatever experiences I'd had with podcasts and I let him know he had been on one or two as a guest already. Jay is a brilliant guy, some would even say genius. He would have figured the podcast thing out on his own. But he had no problem admitting he didn't know quite enough at the time and wanted to pick the brain of someone who did. That's how people like him stay on top. That's true in the media game and in the world in general. If you want to stay great, you need to keep learning.

We look at the Jays, the Tylers, and the Steves as masters of their crafts. And deservedly so. But what they really are are students. Pupils of the game who never stop looking to learn.

Unfortunately, younger generations have a lot of misconceptions about their older peers. One of the biggest is that at some point they "check out," or stop putting in the work.

When you're twenty, you might assume that by the time you're forty you'll somehow have "made it" and can put your life on cruise control. You could even be forty and think that when you hit sixty you'll stop looking for the next adventure, or next come-up.

But what I've thankfully learned through these incredible associates is that the greats *never* stop. They *never* get satisfied. They never stop searching. Which is, of course, such a large part of what made them great in the first place.

Look at Steve Harvey. That guy made more money in his fifties than most people will make in their entire careers, let alone their twenties or thirties. He started on *Family Feud* after fifty, started investing in agriculture after fifty, and started hosting *Miss America* after fifty too. Not because he needed more money, but because he was invigorated by the challenge.

Please never make the mistake of thinking that just because someone is a few generations older than you there's nothing worthwhile for you to talk about with them. No, those are exactly the kind of conversations you need to be having!

What's so frustrating is that we live in an era when these elders are more accessible to us than ever. I understand that not everyone can reach out to a Bishop Jakes or an Arsenio Hall. But you can damn sure reach out to them on social media. You can post questions on their page, send them DMs, tag them with ideas you'd like to hear their perspectives on. Sure, you probably won't hear back in most cases, but even just one reply from someone like that could potentially change your direction in life.

Despite that accessibility, I don't see too many examples of younger folks trying to strike up intergenerational conversations. For instance, I'd love to see a Sylvia Rhone or a Smokey Robinson start to pop up on more of these music podcasts hosted by millennials. They'd have so many incredible gems to share that still hold real value.

Just like I'd love to see a John Hope Bryant, or a Janice Bryant How-royd (the founder of ActOne, the first black woman–led company to gross a billion dollars in revenue) on these millennial finance podcasts. They would elevate the conversations to the highest levels.

The problem is, millennials often aren't looking for dialogue. They're looking for viral moments. And these OGs aren't interested in starting public beefs or needlessly talking mess about folks. They're only interested in sharing hard-won experience and knowledge. Younger folks are so busy chasing "moments" that they've lost sight of the true gems they could be picking up.

I have seen rare moments where people seem to understand the value of this kind of dialogue. One that stands out is the question that went viral a few years back: What would you pick? $500k or a dinner with Jay-Z?

A lot of people said Jay, which shows that they understood the potential impact of learning from him (though Jay himself said that people should take the money!).

Some might say this is another example of America's obsession with celebrity, but if you are a person who has read Jay's book *Decoded*, and watched all his interviews because you truly appreciate how his brain works, then a face-to-face conversation with him *would* be way more valuable than $500k. I'll give you an example why: I recently had a meeting with a president of a major TV network. It wasn't a pitch meeting, the person just wanted to connect with me. If something came out of it, great, but if not, that's cool too. I came in with no expectations, but I ended up being deeply fulfilled by the conversation we had. It was almost like in that moment the person needed to vent and I understood all their frustrations. I walked away feeling I learned so much. Learning from someone with so much experience is invaluable to me. I often prefer that kind of conversation over the money conversations because those are the dialogues that can lead to even more money down the road.

The Jay-Z dinner debate was a great moment, but I'd love to see more like it. And I'd also encourage people to start thinking of the importance of having those conversations with not only folks that are older, but those outside of their cultural comfort zones too.

A lot of young African-Americans appreciated the value of talking with Jay because they could see themselves in him. It's always great to connect with people who come from backgrounds like yours, but it's just as important to push yourself out of that comfort zone. Don't only recognize the value of a conversation with someone who feels familiar like Jay. See the value in the unfamiliar too!

As I mentioned in the Introduction, some of the greatest cross-generational conversations I've had have been with Judy Blume, an eighty-five-year-old Jewish woman who lives in Florida. She wrote some of my favorite books of my childhood, classics like *Blubber* and *Tales of a Fourth Grade Nothing*. I can talk with her for hours, and every time I do, I come away with several jewels that I can apply to my life.

Charlamagne and Judy Blume might not be a friendship you had on your bingo card, but I promise you I cherish each and every moment, and conversation, I have with her.

Looking back, I feel Judy is the person who made me start thinking about the importance of storytelling. The person who made me understand that words, whether written or spoken, had the power to impact lives. Her books always tackled tough topics—like racism, eating disorders, insecurity, and depression—in a humorous and human way. I saw they could change people's lives, and I wanted to learn how to use my words in a similar way.

So anytime Judy makes herself available to me, I'm there. I've already traveled down to Key West twice to hang out with her and her incredible husband, George Cooper. Judy was even gracious enough to let me post one of our conversations on YouTube.

I started that conversation by saying, "My dream interview is happening. You know, every time I get asked what my dream interview is, I always say Judy Blume."

Consider that statement. My dream interview wasn't with a popular rapper, contemporary media figure, or entrepreneur, which is what a lot of folks probably assumed.

No, my dream interview was with a woman who is forty years my senior.

In our conversation, Judy spoke about being rejected by publishers for two years straight before her first book finally sold. Seems hard to believe that someone whose books have changed countless lives would hear no so many times, but that's what Judy encountered. "The first rejection sent me into the closet, sitting on the floor and crying," she told me. "[But] then I said, 'They don't really know what I can do. So let's see what I can do.' And I keep going that way. A lot of success depends on determination. Yes, talent is great when it's time to write, but it's the determination that makes the difference. . . ."

Think about that. Judy Blume's books have sold ninety million copies over her career. But she would have never sold a single one if she stayed feeling down about herself. Her determination and belief in herself is what picked her up and pushed her forward.

Recently I was rewatching the interview and I noticed this comment under the video:

Was slaving away at a script I've been working on that I'm trying to submit to get a literary agent. This interview came at the right time. Work hard and your dreams will manifest!

Seeing that comment made me so happy. Because that's the sort of inspiration we get when we listen to, and communicate with, older generations. Sure, hearing that determination is a key ingredient in success probably doesn't even seem particularly profound. But sometimes hearing that message from someone who actually put that theory into practice is what makes it sink in.

Your peers can post inspirational messages and quotes all day long, but those messages don't hit as hard as the ones from folks who have actually proven these truths to be true. Hearing that Judy Blume got rejected by publishers for two years straight is like hearing that Michael Jordan got cut from his high school basketball team. If these GOATs encountered adversity on their journeys, then we're all going to encounter it. We've just got to push through.

And listen, not every message from an OG or GOAT is going to resonate with younger generations. A few Christmases ago, Judy sent me an autographed copy of *Are You There, God? It's Me, Margaret*, which was recently turned into an incredible movie. Of course I gave it to my daughter. It was time to welcome her into the world of Judy Blume.

But my daughter did not like it! I really wanted to get her blood tested after that. No way *my* daughter doesn't love Judy Blume. "You're not gonna tell me this book don't hold up!" I told her. But she was adamant. For whatever reason, she couldn't connect with it.

But I do everything in my power to make sure she stays engaged in cross-generational conversation. I don't have a lot of folks over to my house, but the ones I do are people I really value and respect. And I make sure that whenever they are over, my kids interact with them. They don't come over, say hi, and then run back to their rooms. No, they hang with us. They get involved in the conversations, even get into debates.

And I love it. Because I know that there's so much more to be found in those conversations than they'll find scrolling on their phones.

We've got to keep these conversations alive.

Let's discuss. . . .

CHAPTER 15

Small Minds

There's not many of us who *think* we're associating with small-minded people. We don't see ourselves as being surrounded by folks with small minds, low expectations, and even lower frequencies.

But we so often *are*.

They're *everywhere*. In our families. Our friend groups. Our jobs. And definitely in our feeds.

Sometimes even in our beds.

No matter who you are, where you live, or what you do, you've got some small-minded people in your circle.

And if you want to avoid small talk taking over your life, then the first step you must take is to remove those small-minded people from it.

It's not even hard. You begin by listening to your body.

Energy, vibrations, intuition, spidey sense—doesn't matter what you call it, it's a thing within you, something you *feel*. You just need to pay attention to it.

You know it's true because it's easy to identify the people whose energy uplifts you. That person who, when you speak to them, you feel better just being around them. They make you see possibilities when before you just saw dead ends. They make you rethink ideas you used to take for granted. They get you excited about things that used to bore you. You might only meet them once, but you'll never forget them.

Then there are people in your life who make your energy go down. Who deflate you the second you begin to feel excited. Who love to point out obstacles. Who make you question your dreams.

Unfortunately, your interactions with those negative sorts of folks are probably much more frequent than your interactions with the people who make you feel inspired. You probably encounter one of those small-minded people almost every day.

Remember the "De-Motivational Speaker" I used to pride myself on being? That's the kind of unhelpful person I'm describing.

So when you start to get those deflated, doubting, and even depressed feelings after talking to someone, take note of it! Don't say, "Oh, she just didn't want me to get my hopes up too high," or "Ah, he just didn't want me to waste my time on something that wasn't going to happen. . . ."

No, that person was trying to make you think small. They wanted to bring you down to the same level they're at.

Acknowledge how they made you feel and then start to change, or even limit, how much interaction you have with that person.

Think of it as like being on a diet. When you're trying to lose some weight, there are certain foods that you have to stay away from. Carbs. Sweets. High-fructose corn syrup. What's the best way to make sure you don't eat what you shouldn't be eating? Keep the bad food out of your house. Keep it out of your life. You have to throw the cookies in the trash, toss the Doritos right after the cookies, and pour the soda down the sink.

The less you see it, the less you'll want it. And the less you want it, the less you'll eat it. Out of sight, out of mind. And in turn, you'll be eating healthier without much effort at all.

It's the same with people. You know these types. You might be sitting at home trying to figure out ways to keep your cholesterol down or your blood pressure in check, and here come so-and-so calling with their junk-food conversation, trying to get you to start consuming garbage again.

And the truth is that small-minded people can come in all shapes and sizes. I have people in my life who are brilliant intellectuals, but even they still get stuck on the small stuff.

It sucks, because when I see their name pop up on my phone, I'll think they're calling to talk about something serious, like whether Congress should vote to raise the debt limit, or how to lower consumer drug prices. I can't wait to get educated and informed.

Instead they'll be calling to talk about whether Cardi and Offset cheated on each other again, or Lil Baby unfollowing Gunna on Instagram (if you're reading this and have no idea who any of those people are, don't worry and please do not waste time "doing your Googles," because we have bigger issues to discuss).

I'm expecting to get intellectually enriched and instead I find myself in a heated hour-long debate about rap drama. When I hang up the phone, I don't feel enriched. I feel drained.

Even if it's someone I respect, if that becomes the type of conversation they're bringing me on a regular basis, then I've got to limit my exposure to them.

It's critical that you be very intentional with your conversations. In *The Four Agreements*, Don Miguel Ruiz stresses that you must "be impeccable with your word." There are a lot of ways you can interpret that statement, but in this context it means don't be wasteful with your conversations. Chatting on and on about celebrities with your buddies is the opposite of impeccable. If having a deep, meaningful conversation is the equivalent of wearing a sharp three-piece suit, then celeb talk is the equivalent of wearing a ratty T-shirt, stained sweatpants with your butt hanging out, and worn-out slides. Not how you want to present yourself to the world.

Listen, are there times when you've got to run out on an errand real quick and the T-shirts and sweats are going to have to do? Sure. But you *limit* how often you wear those outfits. You don't wear them to work, or dates, or to pick your kids up from school (OK, some of us definitely do that).

So give yourself one shallow, celebrity-driven, nonsense conversation a week. That quick run to the store. But then put a cap on it! Once you've had your fun, that's it! And if you find yourself going back to it again that week, think of that nasty T-shirt. Remember, "I need to be impeccable." Or at least presentable.

The easiest way to maintain that weekly limit is to surround yourself with folks who are always focused on the macros, the bigger conversations. They can't make mindless small talk even if they try.

Keep these people close.

I'm going to say it louder for the people in the back.

KEEP THESE PEOPLE CLOSE!!!

And make sure you are reciprocating that energy, because your relationship with individuals like them is beyond valuable.

Just as I spoke above about academically brilliant people who like to talk with me about dumb things, I'm even more thankful there are quite a few people in my life who are always ready to take on big ideas. They're more focused on solutions than drama.

One of my favorite people to discuss real-world issues with is the great Aaron McGruder. Yes, *that* Aaron McGruder. Creator of the classic animated comic strip and TV series *The Boondocks*. I believe *The Boondocks* is one of the greatest shows ever made. The first three seasons of that show, I'll put them up against anything—*The Wire*, *The Sopranos*, whatever.

And the reason why Aaron is so good to talk about real-world issues with is because he comes at it from the angle of satirist. Compared to the average person, his lens is so much wider. A lot of times he even makes *me* feel like the way I'm looking at something is so small compared to how he might see it.

In the next chapter, I'm going to give you a glimpse of what a big talk between Aaron and me looks like.

And we're gonna discuss one of my favorite topics: POLITICS.

The political arena is literally filled with nonsense on both sides. And it's done deliberately by the politicians, manipulating the media (at least some parts of it), to keep you, the average citizen, uninformed and totally uneducated. Because the less you actually know, the less you'll really care.

There's even a term for it, coined by the right-wing operative (and Trump's homeboy) Steve Bannon. It's called "flooding the zone with shit." The more they can keep you flooded in shit, the easier it is for them to get away with all kinds of nefarious things.

And man, are we swimming in shit these days.

In our world, we can reduce it to what it is—small talk. And it's these distractions, this small talk, that keep us away from what we actually should be discussing: the death of democracy as we know it.

Enter my good friend Aaron McGruder.

Let's discuss. . . .

CHAPTER 16

Death of a Nation, Featuring Aaron McGruder

I first became aware of *The Boondocks* through *The Source* magazine in 1997; shortly afterward, it started appearing in newspapers across the country, at which point it turned into a serious cultural force.

When we say representation matters, *The Boondocks* is a prime example. Even though I was always a fan of newspaper comic strips like *Peanuts, Garfield, Calvin and Hobbes, The Far Side,* and *Dilbert,* none of those comics were Black. *The Boondocks* was not only Black. It was *Blackity, Black, Black!!!* Black like the names Tyrone and Jerrell!! (RIP my brother Jerrell Garnett.) The characters Huey Freeman, Riley Freeman, and Michael Caesar all represented myself or other brothers that I knew growing up Black in America. Even better, *The Boondocks* was intellectually stimulating while at the same time it spoke about things that were socially redeeming.

There was Huey and Caesar speaking to the negative influence BET was having on the minds of the youth. Just like there was the period after 9/11 when Huey let everyone know George W. Bush was the spoiled son of a powerful politician from a wealthy oil family supported by religious fundamentalists, who had no respect for the democratic electoral process, bombed innocents, and used war to deny people their civil liberties. In other words, *The Boondocks* DID NOT DO SMALL TALK. Not in the least bit. I don't think there has ever been anything in mainstream pop culture that has held the mirror up to America—especially Black America—the way *The Boondocks* has.

One of the reasons *The Boondocks* hit so hard was that it addressed macro issues without making them too complex. *The Boondocks'* secret weapon was good ol'-fashioned common sense. It's amazing to think about how radical this was then; especially when we consider how rare using common sense is now.

Now, I've always been the type of person to look under the hood. So when I began reading *The Boondocks*, I had to immediately know who the creator was. Soon, I would come to find out it was the brainchild of someone I would later call a friend. His name is Aaron McGruder.

I have to tell you about how I came to know Aaron on a personal level. Like I said, I was a huge fan of the franchise. Whether it was the comic strip, the TV show, the books (from *Because I Know You Don't Read* to *All the Rage*, I had them all), even interviews that Aaron did—I guess you could say I was a McGruder junkie. The same way we would be in these barbershops talking about Lil Baby and Future, that was how I was with *The Boondocks* and Aaron McGruder. You'd have thought I was getting paid to be on his promotional team.

So one day about eighteen years ago, I was talking to a friend named April Bombai. April is from the West Coast. And while I'm sitting there, going on and on about *The Boondocks*, she just casually drops it on me—"Charlamagne, I know Aaron." I'm like, "April stop, *nobody* knows Aaron; he's a recluse. In fact, there's debates in online forums about whether or not he is even a real person."

She swore up and down that Aaron McGruder was, in fact, real. To prove it, she would ask him if it was OK for me to have his email address, and he graciously passed it along. I reached out not long afterward, telling him how big of a fan I was. I didn't expect a response. I thought he would be too busy making TV shows. But lo and behold, he wrote back! This began an ongoing series of correspondence, and in 2008 we met in person at a party for the Cartoon Network's Adult Swim.

Still, it wasn't until ten years later that Aaron and I really became friends. That was when he began reaching out to me to discuss life, society, politics, and so much else that was going on in the world. At the time, Aaron was getting back into creating *Boondocks* content. He'd taken a hiatus and now he had a new series of strips he'd created.

Of course, being the huge fan that I am, I was thrilled when we decided that I would release those new *Boondocks* strips on my Instagram page. Predictably, these strips went extremely viral and, in turn, Aaron ended up doing a deal for a *Boondocks* movie and cartoon with HBO Max that I was fortunate enough to be made a consulting producer on. Aaron didn't have to do any of that for me, but he did. Likewise, I ended up making him an executive producer on my late-night talk show on Comedy Central. We've been locked in ever since.

Aaron is a person who truly focuses on the macros and not the micros. To give you an example of how he tackles an issue, I will now cede the floor to Aaron McGruder to discuss Donald Trump and white supremacy. . . .

I want to start off talking about a subject matter I'm never going to shut up about: white supremacy.

White supremacy is kryptonite for white folks. They're powerless against it. Russians, Indians, Islamic terrorists—America is so strong against every other enemy. But white supremacy, we've never had an answer for.

Why?

Because it's in our country's DNA.

We have the tools to stop this, we had them a long time ago.

We—or, I should say, they—chose not to choose them, though. And that's what got us here.

I think it's because, even if they have the tools, white men can't imagine doing it to themselves. So, it's almost nonvoluntary; this idea of going hard after a powerful white man—trying to take them down, so to speak—is just not shit they do. That's why I think you see, over the last several years, the nation struggling with these weak or sometimes nonexistent efforts to stop this from happening, even though it's been happening in slow motion for so long.

Whether it's in government, law enforcement; white men can't defend themselves, against themselves. It's a blind spot. Donald Trump represents the worst of themselves, and obviously there are a lot of white people who don't like Donald Trump, but he's still one of them. He's their cousin, their brother, their idiot uncle.

On the flip side, Black people can really hate racists. We can really hate white supremacy. White people can dislike it, they can know, in their heart, that it's fucked up. But Black people, we can totally hate it. Even the best, most purest, most honest, most well-to-do, good-natured, bake you some cookies and bring them over to you on Easter Sunday kind of white person, is never going to hate their racist-ass uncle or cousin the way a Black person hates them. That white person may dislike 'em, they can disapprove; but they're never going to hate 'em like we do. Because of the blind spot—that inability to completely and totally not fuck with another white person.

The best white man has their racist uncle and their racist cousin, and they can't hate them the way we hate them. And so, in the grand scheme of what America is in terms of the rich and powerful and privilege, even if he's a bum, even if he's a broke bum . . . you know, there've been other white men too who've been able to pull off that con. He's one of them.

I remember when Robert Mueller was investigating Donald Trump and the Russian collusion theory of the 2016 presidential election. *The media would juxtapose Trump and Mueller. "These people couldn't be more different: Robert Mueller and Donald Trump." But it's like, no, they're the same. They show up at the same get-togethers, they run in the same circles . . . this is who they are. The ones the establishment wants to hold in esteem, like the Reagans and the Bushes versus the Trumps and the low-lifes, they're all one family. They're one type. So, they can't hate themselves as much as we despise them. They can't see it. It's like putting your face too close to a mirror. When you're that close, you can't see anything the way it really is.*

Rich, powerful, white Americans. That's a culture in this country. It's legitimately an identity. You know how some folks identify as L, G, B, T, or Q. Some people identify as rich, powerful, and white. And those people really have a hard time going after their own.

Obviously, on a micro level, there is a lot of disagreement among white people. They don't all have consensus on their white supremacy—even though, no matter what they do, it upholds white supremacy.

Case in point, you got the Republicans and the Democrats. Republicans don't do shit for poor white people, but poor white people stay voting Republican. You could say they're voting against their own self-interest, but in a way, they're not. They vote Republican because if they were to vote Democrat, niggas would benefit. And if Black people are going to benefit, it's not going to fly. Everything— and I do mean everything—is viewed through that lens.

Take the federal government. Republicans hate the federal government. Why? Because they took away white people's place. You can dress it up in all kinds of high-minded talk about "states' rights." Believe me, it ain't that. It's that the federal government gave Black people their civil rights. And white people are still mad about it.

I use the word "culture" a lot. I think it's key to understanding politics, because cultures are bigger than individuals. Cultures change over decades, not months and weeks. Culture outlasts everything. So in terms of that, this hatred of anything that also helps Black people is woven into the white man's culture. They just have to be better than Black people.

To them, this might as well be a game. White people play it against Black people. They also play it against themselves. The wealthy whites play the poor whites every damn day. They do it because it has always worked.

White people love to lie to white people about other white people. Look at Fox News. That's just a media network that is doing the same shit white people were doing a hundred years ago, when the rich, powerful Southern white man was lying to the poor Southern white man about what the Northern white man was doing.

The whites up north, they're helping the niggas, they'd say. Now the poor Southern white doesn't fuck with the Northern white, because he hears about welfare and all these social programs, and he thinks all this stuff is true. Meanwhile, the rich Southern white man is happy as hell. Nobody's asking him for nothing. So long as he keeps that Northern white man out of power, the Southerner doesn't have to do shit. If the poor white gets angry, it ain't at him. It's never directed at the rich white man who's been exploiting him this whole time. It's always at the Democrats, who in their mind are helping the niggas.

The system I just described has been in place forever in this country. You can turn your TV on right this very second and Fox News probably has some variation of this argument about Joe Biden. It never changes.

Their disposition is always the same. Republicans create the conditions for anyone to get rich. And Democrats are going to take your hard-earned money and just give it to some Black people. Race will always be at the core of this dynamic. It's always about Joe Biden helping niggas. Federal government helping niggas. Culturally, Republicans see themselves as the opposite of that, and they always will. They always will.

The political right is grounded in Black suffering. They won't let that go. They feel like if Black people aren't suffering, they're doing something wrong in life. In their minds, they just wanna see themselves win. But when you look at Black people as a potential threat, like a pest, you wanna make sure the fly gets swatted. That's suffering.

Those things are intrinsically connected. They cannot feel like they're winning if Black people somewhere aren't being punished, and kept in line, and kept in check. A lot of times that expresses itself in very brutal and very immediate ways, like a racist police force. But it also expresses itself in the high-minded debate about money, finance, and a social safety net.

No matter how you do the math, it always adds up to a brutal attack on Black people. That's the end result. No matter what they say it's about, it's really just: we don't like these niggas and we can't imagine sharing prosperity with them.

Now, people love to talk about separation of church and state in this country, but there's always been a state religion in America, and it's not Christianity—it's White Supremacy.

The insurrection on January 6, 2021, is such a strong example of the power of this religion. A bunch of predominantly white folks traveled to Washington, DC, because they believed some niggas in Atlanta and Detroit were up to no good. That's all it took. Because that belief is central to their faith. "These niggas must've been up to no good" is their definition of inner city Black people. With them, that concept has so much cultural resonance. More than George Washington and Santa Claus, it's literally something they can believe in.

The details don't even matter. "Niggas up to no good" is all the evidence they need. Meanwhile, actual issues with voter fraud and voter ID do not exist. It is a nonexistent thing. But their religion requires that they all agree to pretend it is. It's a cultural thing. And this goes all the way back to the Confederacy.

Same people that tried to end the country in 2021 are the ones who tried to end it in the 1860s. Biologically, I have to assume some of these people are actually related. Same folks. Doing the same shit. And they're going to keep doing it. Because they've gamed the political system to where they, the right wing, essentially have minority rule. You couldn't do it without people like Mitch McConnell, you know, stealing Supreme Court seats from a Black president. It takes a lot of capitulation, a lot of lackadaisicalness, I guess, to allow this to happen.

And in so much of right-wing politics, racism is just the unspoken center of gravity. No one ever refers to Mitch McConnell stealing the Supreme Court seat from a Black president as a racist act, but it was. You wouldn't have robbed a white man like that. You did that to a Black president. That's a hate crime. But no one ever talks about it in that way.

But anyway, it happened. And now we are here.

Every single thing that's happening in this country today—the rise of Trump, January 6th—is a response to Barack Obama. It was a perfect storm. Donald Trump was a cultural icon. I mean, it's crazy to think of him that way, but he was. Then he entered a party of Republicans that was extremely weakened. Nobody even remembers Jeb Bush and Marco Rubio. It was like, these mother-fuckers are losers.

But then that perfect storm turns into an aggressive white cultural movement, harkening back to the days of sacking Washington and breaking the Republic. Quite literally.

And Donald Trump's rise really destroyed the illusion that it was ever about anything but racism. You had these lost, ex-Republicans on MSNBC and CNN, like "I don't know what happened." You don't know what happened? Racism happened. You thought it was about some other shit. That was the problem with the Republicans. They lost the plot. Racism, it was always about racism.

I mean, think about it. Even when we talk about January 6th. We don't really talk about white supremacist insurrection as sort of the center-motivating thing. Basically, white people were trying to invalidate the votes of millions of Black people.

And white people were the only ones who could have stormed the Capitol. Nobody else would have even tried. Think about how many layers of protection, how many layers of law enforcement, had to stand down in order for that to happen. That's something you'd never see happening if it was a bunch of Black people trying to get up in there.

For such a strong, powerful country to be so vulnerable, it's very interesting. If you think of the country as an organism with an immune system, this must be how cancer works. Something feels too familiar and the body can't attack it soon enough and it grows into something awful. That's what we're living through and that's what, in the storming of the Capitol, we saw playing out. It would take something really strong and powerful to change that. It would take real leadership, and using the tools that are available for democracy to defend itself against this kind of thing.

But to extend our scope further, this cancer has infected everyone, not just people in America.

Think about what's happened with Russians. Until America elected a Black president, white Americans hated Russians. I don't know why, exactly. Maybe mothafuckers just watched Rocky IV *too many times. But I remember, growing up, thinking, "Wow the* white American man hates the white Russian man. They're white, he's white, why don't they get along?"

Then Obama got elected. And a lot of those very same people were like, whoa, wait up there a second, these Russians ain't so bad. They might have felt a little less cool about the Russians after Putin invaded Ukraine, but still, it wasn't like, I hate you Russian motherfuckers! It was like, wow, you invaded Ukraine, that's terrible, you probably shouldn't do that.

But all around the world, after Obama, I think a lot of democratic countries saw the rise of right-wing nationalism, where there was hatred of their own internal ethnic minorities, and a pushback against immigrants. There was this commonality that they saw among themselves as white people, finally. It was like, you believe in capitalism, I believe in communism, but fuck it, we're both white, and whatever we do, we can't let those people get into power.

All in all, I think the solution to some of these problems is that we need to stop spending so much time worrying about how white people feel. The threat to democracy is institutional. White supremacy is at the very core of the country. Real leadership and real action aren't about what anyone is saying to the public. It's about shoring up the institutions and moving aggressively to purge this shit. If there's an insurrectionist, they should be purged.

But the problem is, everything in this country is centered around how it makes white people feel. Like, if it's going to offend white people, they can't do it. In turn, we fail to defend ourselves. There's probably a lot of people in the United States military who are sympathetic to the insurrectionist movement. But it's a political issue to filter them out.

You even have people here who say stuff like "What you call white supremacist, I call American." It's some funny shit. I say it's funny because it's about perspective. What I call white supremacy, they call "self-interest." You don't have to wake up and think of yourself as a Nazi so much as wake up and, in your world, expect things to be a certain way.

And niggas don't belong in that world. That's just it. Maybe they think about them, maybe they don't. But they definitely don't wanna spend no money on 'em. And they definitely don't want 'em nowhere near them. And they wanna make sure they have a strong police force to control their movements and behaviors. Then they make up their own ghost stories about them and believe them.

That's the animating principle. That's "white supremacy."

Let's discuss. . . .

CHAPTER 17

Talkin' Loud and Sayin' Somethin'

My Pops was obsessed with James Brown. That man was his favorite musical artist, bar none. Maybe it was because James was
unapologetically Black and proud. Maybe it was because James
was born in Barnwell, South Carolina. Maybe it was because he
loved cocaine and had a lot of women on the side. Whatever the
reason, my father was the founder and CEO of the James Brown
Stan Club.

My father was so serious about James Brown that he dressed like
he might get called up on stage to perform alongside James Brown at
any given moment. Red jacket, red pants, red shoes, and a red hat. All
leather of course. That sort of look that you have to rock to run James
Brown's Stan Club.

My father loved all the music James made, but one of his absolute
favorites was the classic "Talkin' Loud and Sayin' Nothin'."

So in honor of both my father and the Godfather of Soul, I've named
this chapter "Talkin' Loud and Sayin' Somethin'"!

Talking loud can attract a lot of attention. But most loud talkers,
like James tried to warn us, are saying a whole bunch of nothing.

I used to fall into that category. When I first got on the radio in
South Carolina, I wasn't just a talker, or even just a loud talker—I was
a yeller and a screamer.

I could be reporting the weather, sharing the traffic, or introducing a record—it didn't matter. I yelled everything I said.

I'd do it at different times in the day too. Morning drive, afternoon shift, late nights—I was shouting everything. Didn't help that the most popular slang at the time was HOLLA! Because I damn sure did a lot of hollering. . . .

It wasn't that I had anything particularly important to say, I just didn't know there were different ways to get my point across. I was just one of the young and the reckless. Brash and ambitious and I thought the literal volume of my voice should reflect my internal energy.

Luckily, a radio OG named George Cook pulled me aside and set me straight. "You know, you'll connect with more people if you have a conversational tone instead of yelling," George told me. "Don't be DMX all the time. You can be LL Cool J too."

Putting it in rapper terms really helped me understand George's point. DMX was incredible (RIP to the DOG), but even DMX knew when to have a conversational tone. You heard it in records like "Slippin'" and "How's It Goin' Down." Adding that conversational coolness really expanded my repertoire.

Big George taught me how to pick my spots with my voice. How there were times where it made sense to be hyped (usually 7 p.m. to 10 p.m.), and other times (after 11 p.m., when I was playing slow songs in a segment I called "Thug Love Status") where a calm, level, conversational tone was actually the best way to get your point across.

That's a lesson that I've tried to carry with me off the air and into my life.

Don't get me wrong, there are still times that I raise my voice. I am pretty naturally loud and so are ALL my daughters. So there are times when I amp it up, but only when I want to deliver an important message.

I recently had to raise my voice while I was taping my hall of fame radio show *The Breakfast Club*. Not at a guest, or a caller, as you might have expected, but at our staff. Because there was a message I needed to make sure the staff heard.

I promise you, unlike the younger version of me who was too turned up, I am very laid back when we are recording *The Breakfast Club*. First of all, we start the show at 6 a.m. every morning and I was born in 1900 and 78. I'm officially an oldhead. I can't waste my energy talking loud if I ain't saying nothin'.

Also, I'm much more secure in myself and how I communicate with people now than when I was a young man. I'm not as thirsty to get my point across, because (depending on the subject) I KNOW I'm right. I try to let my actions speak louder than my voice.

But on this occasion, I felt like I had to raise the volume just a little bit. For a show that reaches millions of people each day, it's recorded in a very laid-back, family-like environment. When you have to be at work at 6 a.m. everyday, you tend to let your hair down a little.

But every now and then folks get too relaxed.

The way the show works is that when we cut to commercials, we'll often record segments and promos that can be run later in the show. That frees up time for us to start taping interviews for the next day's episode. (Surprise! We don't do interviews "live.")

Once we pretape a segment, it's up to our producers and staff to insert the appropriate segment later in the show. On this particular day, I was in the studio with my co-host DJ Envy talking while the "live to tape" show played in the background. While we were talking, I heard one of the worst things you can possibly hear as a radio personality:

A curse word.

Someone had forgotten to edit it out of the segment. Not just any curse word, but the BIG F. I'm talking about the one that rhymes with stuck, luck, buck, and suck. In their cars, or on their computers, in their kitchens—wherever people listen to the show—all they were hearing was FUCK.

I looked out of the studio's windows and expected to see the staff looking like they were in the middle of a fire drill, trying to figure out how to fix things. Instead, I saw . . . nothing. Not a soul was even paying attention, they were laughing, talking, scrolling Instagram. Not even realizing they might have just cost us millions of dollars in fines. They were doing everything except listening to the actual radio show they were supposed to be creating. Producers, videographers, interns— no one was listening.

As the host, I should be the last person who catches a mistake like that. Instead, I was the *only* person who caught it.

Folks had gotten too comfortable. This wasn't the first time something like this had happened. I had been noticing the attention to detail slipping over the prior few months. Prep questions not properly researched. Dead air sometimes. Wrong audio clips being played while we were discussing certain topics on-air. But nothing as egregious as a BIG FAT *FUCK* on-air. So I decided at that moment it was time to raise the volume a little bit.

As SOOOOOONNN as we went off the air, I gathered the entire staff in the studio.

I let them know that "What happened earlier today isn't acceptable. We are one of the top radio programs in the country, but we are also one of the worst-produced radio programs in the country. We reach millions of people a day. We are syndicated in over one hundred markets."

People were staring at me. I had their undivided attention so I had to tell them exactly how I felt: "Look, I *care*," I said looking around the room. "But *I don't give a fuck*."

See, there is a difference between not caring and not giving a fuck.

I care because I want everyone in that room who has the privilege of working on that show to be great and go on to do incredible things in the game of radio. But I also don't give a fuck whether they listen to me or not. If they're not committed to being great, I'll just get some people in there who actually do their job at a high level and continue on about my life.

To be clear, I wasn't screaming. I wasn't yelling. I was talking at a conversational level. If we had been in a crowded restaurant, you might not have even been able to hear me. But it was still a *loud* conversation. I was putting people on alert.

I felt comfortable being loud because, as I told the staff, I do care. I care about them, and I care about the show. Very deeply. I'd rather raise my voice and grab their attention than quietly let them drift until they reach a point there's no coming back from.

I don't particularly like doing it, but if I am going to talk like that, it will be to say something important. And something I intend to back up.

Have you ever heard the expression "Talk softly but carry a big stick"? It's generally taken to mean you don't need to speak at a high volume, or shout, to get your point across. But you do need to be prepared to back up your softly spoken words with action.

It's a quote that's often attributed to the US president Theodore Roosevelt. But in the letter the quote is taken from, President Roosevelt actually says that it's a West African proverb. So given my West African ancestry, maybe I just come by my "speak softly but carry a big stick" energy naturally!

Unfortunately, it's an energy that not everyone seems to have. Talking loud is a problem across the board, but one area where the volume has really gotten too high is media.

I'm not talking about the shows—on radio, podcasts, and everywhere else—themselves. I think there are a lot of truly wonderful shows that really help keep people entertained, informed, and inspired. Shows like *The Pivot, The Read, Deeply Well with Devi Brown, Woman Evolve with Sarah Jakes Roberts, 85 South Show, Carefully Reckless with Jess Hilarious*, just to name a few.

But more specifically, I'm referring to how some folks in the business talk about any kind of "nontraditional" media. I don't know if it's because it's a relatively new industry, but I've noticed that the people in that space, especially in the hip-hop podcasting space, like to talk a little too loudly about their success.

Recently I was down in Philadelphia speaking at a podcasting conference put on by Wallo, one half of the *Million Dollaz Worth of Game* podcast. Wallo and his partner, Gillie, are a great example of successful podcasters who talk loudly, but in an encouraging and instructional way. More podcasters need to follow their example.

Which is why at the conference I made the point to share a simple message when asked, "What advice do you have for people trying to break into podcasting?" My answer? "We don't need more podcasters, we need electricians, welders, plumbers, folks who know how to fix a roof. Air conditioners too." There are too many podcasters and 95 percent of them are not saying *shit*. And to be fair, this applies to streamers, YouTubers, and all kinds of influencers—most of them are just talking to hear themselves at this point. Talking loud and not saying a damn thing. That might work for a moment, but it's not a recipe for any sort of lasting success.

My other message was that podcasters need to stop ranting about whatever sort of financial successes they're claiming to have. Because chances are they're lying. And for who?

Lying at the top of your lungs about how much money you're making, that's small talk I absolutely hate.

In fact, let me pull back the curtain and tell you how this game really works. I want to show you some industry math real quick. Let's say you get a check for $3.1 million. I'm just using this as an example to show you what that $3.1 really looks like. Because even a check that big isn't really as life-altering as you might think.

Number one, Uncle Sam is taking 45 percent of that off the jump. That's almost $1.2 million for him to use on God knows what. Then you'll pay another $500k in commissions. Lawyers, agents, manager, business partner, they all gotta eat too. I can't complain about that—those people worked very hard to make the deal happen. They deserve their cut. So you left with about $1.2 million bucks. That's incredible. You should never not be excited about getting a check for that size. But it is a big difference from a check for $3.1 million. That money goes a long way for me, because as I've said, I don't have a taste for exotic cars, jewelry, etc. I live very much within my means. But if I didn't live within my means, a check like that could basically be gone by the time it hit my account because people want to look like they have money as opposed to actually having it. This is why I know so many folks out there who claim to be ballin' but are damn near broke.

When you lie about what you're making, or how much of an impact you're having, you're not just making a fool out of yourself in the long run, you're also messing up everyone else's expectations. That's another gem I shared at Wallo's PodCon. Don't just lower your voice, lower your expectations. You're making too many people on the right path feel like they're anything but. The lying, exaggerating, and bragging have a whole bunch of people—especially young people—feeling like their sustainable growth plans are hopeless.

It's gotten to the point where someone could be out here making a solid living, right now, off their podcast and feel like they're losing because they're not quite at the level of posting dripped-out fit pics to IG every day. That's insane to me.

If you can comfortably keep a roof over your head, food on the table, and provide for yourself by talking into a microphone for an hour a week, please understand that you are winning. Big-time.

My mother was a teacher who never made over $30k per year in her entire career. And she definitely worked harder than any podcaster I've ever met. My daddy certainly never earned six figures a year either (at least not legally).

If you're making good money at podcasting, or any job for that matter that you enjoy, be proud of that without throwing it in everyone's face. And whatever you do, please do not loudly talk down to someone else who doesn't seem to be experiencing the same success as you.

Bragging loudly is the worst form of communication. I've never understood the impulse to talk that way.

I've done pretty well for myself, but I've never felt the need to talk down to others about their finances.

Because I know where I've come from. I worked at Taco Bell. I worked at a flower garden. I SOLD CRACK and I got a lisp!!!! Hell I even graduated from night school two years after I was supposed to graduate from high school.

What sense does it make for me to ever talk down to someone else? How is that helping me? And it's definitely not helping them.

And if I do have to speak loudly, it will be with good intentions and love. Let's discuss. . . .

CHAPTER 18

Same-Day Service

A lot of folks talk about gratitude being their priority, but there isn't much gratitude in their actual actions. Which is why in this chapter I want to talk about the importance of service.

I was very fortunate to grow up in a family where being of service was always emphasized. No matter how poor we were I never knew hunger, because my family, especially my grandmother, always found a way to make sure everyone was going to eat. Even if she had to deprive herself, probably even more than we will ever know, she was going to make sure her family was relaxed, happy, and fed when we got together.

My father, in his own way, had a similar mentality. If there was a get-together, Pops was going to make sure everyone had a full drink in their hand (and maybe something stronger) and was having a good time. For a while he ran an under-the-radar (aka illegal) juke-joint type of venue where he'd serve drinks, sell food, and even throw concerts. It was supposed to help him make some extra cash, but he would hand out drinks on the house. I'm sure it impacted his bottom line, but he couldn't help himself. Making sure people were happy was just in his nature.

I'm cut from the same cloth. I genuinely love doing things for people. It's something that makes me happy in life. And no, I'm not going to tell you specifics of what I do because that's not the point (and that'd be bragging, right?). When I didn't have much, I found ways to share. And now that I have a lot, I share a lot too.

But there is one situation I'm OK talking about because it was a reminder to me how even a little gesture of help can go a long way with someone who is struggling. Not too long ago I was at the Roc Nation United Justice Coalition event and a woman came up to me. "Hi," she said. "My name is Nichole Bell." We chatted about the event for a few minutes, until she said, "You probably don't remember it, but you did something very nice for me once." And I'm not afraid to admit that I honestly didn't remember.

She went on to explain that she was the fiancée of Sean Bell, the young man who was senselessly gunned down by the police in Queens the night of his 2006 bachelor party. A year or so after his death I was in a restaurant in Queens and must have recognized her, because apparently I paid for her and her party's bill. I didn't tell her I was doing it, the waiter just told her when they asked for their bill, "Don't worry, Charlamagne was in here too and he already took care of it."

Nikki told me it was just a small gesture, but it meant a lot to her at a time when she had begun to wonder if people had forgotten about her and Sean. It was a small reminder that they hadn't. And she still remembered it all these years later.

To me, the most beautiful thing about having money is that you can give some of it away. It might be picking up someone's dinner bill. It might be helping put someone's child through school. Or paying their rent during a tough time. Or taking care of a funeral for a family that's grieving.

The one time I made a big, public gift was when I gave a $250,000 donation to my Ford Family Endowment Scholarship Fund at South Carolina State University, my mother's alma mater. I never got around to college myself, but I knew how much of a struggle it was for my mother to go to school there and I wanted to help lighten some other people's loads if I could.

I'm happy to give the money away because I already have way more than I need materially. You'll never see me driving a Bentley or Phantom, just like you'll never see me with a bunch of gold around my neck. It's just not me.

If I get a big check, I don't say to myself, "OK, time to buy another car," or "time to put more ice on my wrist." Those thoughts never cross my mind.

I believe that mentality has actually helped keep me sane and balanced. When your focus is on helping others, instead of amassing toys, your ego will never get out of control.

And lending a helping hand keeps me balanced by letting me stay in personal touch with the lived experience of others less fortunate than I have been. I remember very vividly what it was like to be broke. To be envious of what other kids had. To not be able to afford to keep a roof over your head. To have a child that you couldn't properly provide for.

I hated feeling that way. And if I can ease even just a little bit of the struggle of someone that's in a similar situation, then I'm going to do it.

I'm not the first person that grew up in a trailer, or in a housing project, who ended up doing pretty well for themselves. Far from it.

But for some folks from backgrounds like mine, the goals of that money quickly shift to putting up, by spending up, a wall between themselves and the life they used to live. Collecting material things to put distance between who they once were and who they've become. They want to get as far away from the sense of lacking, of neediness, as possible.

I have the opposite mindset. I want to stay as close to who I once was as possible. That doesn't mean I'm going to move my family back into a single-wide trailer, or ride around in a car with 200k miles on it (though I was pushing that 2004 Cadillac Escalade until recently). But I am going to go out of my way to use my wealth to assist someone who could use the help.

I also want to stress that helping someone out doesn't only mean financial assistance either. There are plenty of ways you can put your arm around folks and improve their lives without giving them a dollar.

I certainly benefited from that sort of help in my own career. When I was a radio personality who kept getting fired from jobs I thought I was doing well at, I had folks who would pull me aside and give me advice and encouragement.

They would tell me, "Don't worry about what happened, you have real talent at this. You can be great. Just stay at it."

When you are struggling and doubting your future, hearing that sort of encouragement from people who are already established in the business is priceless. There were times when it was really the only thing that kept me pushing forward. "Maybe this radio thing just isn't for me," I'd think. But then I'd remember, "Nah, the OG said that I had talent for this. In fact, he said I have what it takes to be great." And then I would keep on grinding away.

Knowing how discouraging my industry can be is why I've always tried to help out whenever I see someone talented trying to make their way up the ladder. I remember a time when Nyla Symone, who is now a radio host at Power 105.1, first started interning at the station. I'd been watching her work ethic and was impressed. As someone who's worked in radio for years, you can tell pretty quickly when an intern either has "it" or doesn't have "it." The ones who have it don't need much in the way of instruction. They figure out on their own what needs to be done and then get at it. They're not happy just to be there—they're happy to have an opportunity to make an impression. They're not primarily concerned with asking for tickets to events or free swag or selfies with celebrities, their focus is on finding ways to help the team.

Nyla definitely had "it."

One day, and I'm not making this up, God said to me, "Hey man, that young lady right there, go talk to her. I have an encouraging message I want you to give her." So I walked over to her and said, "Yo, it's gonna sound crazy, but God told me to tell you that everything's gonna be OK, and you just need to find the one thing you want to focus on. And when you do, everything is going to fall into place."

Nyla was definitely shocked by my pronouncement, but she also conceded that I had spoken to the very issue that was keeping her up at night. Unbeknownst to me she was exploring becoming a DJ, one of her true passions. After we spoke, she found the confidence to trust her gut: followed her dream and has quickly became one of the most sought out DJs in the country.

She currently has her own show on Power 105.1 called *Blendz and Trendz*. She has a podcast called *We Need to Talk* that *Essence* magazine said is one of the ten Black podcasts you need to listen to. She has been nominated for DJ of the Year at the BET Awards, Complex named her one of the twenty-five most influential hip-hop media personalities in the game, and she has become such a tastemaker that I started to invite her on *The Breakfast Club* to play some of her favorite new tracks for the audience in a segment we do every Friday called "Pass Da Aux." That segment has turned into a live event called "Certified Vibe" where all the up-and-coming next stars of the game come to perform.

I love when I'm able to provide a service like that. I can also remember when the good brothers Desus and Mero had signed a development deal with MTV, but the network couldn't figure out what to do with them. I'd be having meetings inside the office and Mero would just be wandering around, throwing up graffiti on the walls in his office.

Well, if Viacom didn't know what to do with them, I sure did. I was about to launch my MTV2 show *Uncommon Sense,* so I said, "Yo, let's give them a segment every week. They'll kill it." And they did!

I was able to get so many up-and-coming talents a platform through that show. Desus and Mero. Zuri Hall. Taxstone. Crissle West. Kazeem Famuyide. Cardi B. Chico Bean. Karlous Miller. DC Young Fly.

I'm not saying I discovered any of those folks. They were all already doing great things. But if I helped elevate their visibility even just a few degrees, then that's something I can look back on and be very proud about.

Elevating people's visibility isn't even something I consciously think about. For me, it's literally like breathing. I'm always looking for who's next and how I can help them.

Who can I amplify? That's my position in the game. To help amplify talent.

Some people grow to great heights themselves, but their tree doesn't bear much fruit. That could never be me. If I don't use my success to put others in position, then I've failed.

And it's not because I'm so altruistic, or have such a big heart. There's a selfish reason for it too. When you don't put people on and help grow them, you are putting a ceiling on your own legacy. If you never help anyone else, who's going to sing your praises when you're gone?

When you do help empower others, however, you'll never be forgotten. You'll always have folks recounting the good things you did. Reminding the world of your impact. Maybe it's egotistical to want to be thought of that way. But hey, if having that sort of ego means I'm more inclined to help people, then maybe that's one part of my ego I don't have to kill after all.

It's not just in the media world either. Whether you're in academia, in science, marketing, hospitality—the same rule applies! If you see someone who can use some guidance or encouragement, share it with them! Do not worry that by putting someone else on you're somehow weakening your own position.

If anything, just the opposite is true. By putting someone else on, you're creating an ally and friend for life. We always remember the people who gave us a hand, or shared a kind word. Even the smallest gestures stay with us for a lifetime. Think about your own experiences. You can still remember the teachers who said you were smart. The coaches who told you that you could play. The bosses who said they saw your potential. You never forget them.

Being successful just for the sake of being successful is a hollow "victory." Leaders know that true, lasting success—a legacy—can only come through service to others.

Let's discuss. . . .

CHAPTER 19

Ego Strength

The weak are dominated by their ego, the wise dominate their ego, and the intelligent are in a constant struggle against their ego.
—HAMZA YUSUF

Throughout this book I've been promoting open conversation. Encouraging you to engage in meaningful and heartfelt dialogue with the world.

This chapter is different.

This chapter isn't about dialogue. It's about *confrontation*.

Not with your ops. Or your critics.

No, I'm talking about confronting your own ego.

Out of all the running conversations you have in your life, the one that has to have a constant *confrontational* tone is the one you have with your ego.

Because when you let your ego drive, you never reach your destination.

Even worse, you're always bound to crash.

Not just a fender-bender, either. I'm talking about the type of crash where the cops have to get out the jaws of life to save you.

How to avoid that sort of crash was a difficult lesson for me to learn.

There have been plenty of times where I didn't properly challenge my ego. Where I let it take the wheel and was content to go along for the ride.

Needless to say, I didn't like where it took me.

The time my ego was the most out of control was around 2015. *The Breakfast Club* was really starting to take off. For the first time in my career, I wasn't looking over my shoulder anymore.

Instead, I felt like I had *arrived*. I won't lie, the attention got to me.

To be clear, not the way attention gets to a lot of celebrities. I wasn't demanding bowls full of green M&Ms in my dressing room. I wasn't throwing phones at my assistants. I wasn't insisting that no one look me in the eye.

One thing I pride myself on is showing respect to everyone I work with and come into contact with. I always show love. That's just something that's rooted in me. My grandmother always told me that manners will take you where money won't. I've always tried to follow her lead.

Except, ironically, when it came to the person who mattered the most in my life:

My wife.

Like a lot of men, as soon as I got married, I assumed I was ready to hang my playa jersey up in the rafters.

What I wasn't prepared for was that a lot of women still want to deal with you when you're married. Especially when you're experiencing public success.

There's something about that sort of attention that got to my head. Having women know that I was taken, but still come on to me. That made my ego go through the roof.

To be clear, I'm not blaming my cheating on those women. I could have said no.

The blame lies squarely with me. More specifically, with my insecurities.

In the media, I was becoming a big deal. A celebrity. Rubbing shoulders with stars.

But in my mind? I was still that kid in the sixth-grade class picture with the fanny pack and the Coke bottle glasses. Who got bullied every day after school. Who the girls thought was corny. Or ugly. Who none of the girls seemed to like, and it didn't help that a bunch of dudes my age was already fucking.

I became very insecure in middle school that I wasn't having sex yet. Hell, I didn't lose my virginity until tenth grade. (We're not counting the sexual abuse I experienced as a child, right?) That might not seem so late, but compared to my friends, I felt very behind. It left an empty space that I was very conscious of for a long time. Longer than made any sort of rational sense.

So when these women started trying to get with me, even after I was spoken for, it fed into that piece of me that still felt like it was empty. I didn't know how to say no.

My ego was more than happy to jump into that space and scream "YESSSS!" at the top of its lungs.

I was also making content that fed into the perception of me as some kind of wild womanizer. As I mentioned, there was me sniffing J.Lo's chair after she got up (I don't know if that qualifies as "womanizing," but it gives you an idea of where my head—and nose—were at). Or asking the adult film star Mishikato to model her lingerie line for me.

The audience seemed to love it. "Charlamagne's crazy," they'd say. Or "That boy's wild."

They ate it up. But it was also eating me alive.

That's because it wasn't really me. I was pushing a persona I had created in order to make that late bloomer feel like he had finally arrived.

I was able to play the role during the day, but it would always catch up with me at night. Especially when I was lying in bed with my wife. When you turn out the lights next to a person who knows you ain't doing right, you don't sleep so well.

My wife never caught me cheating red-handed (that I know of), but she *knew.* I was living a CIA-level secret life of meetings that lasted way longer than they needed to, business trips that turned to more than business, and phone calls I had to "take outside or in another room," but she wasn't ever truly fooled. She certainly knew that *I* was a fool.

Man, was I ever. If my wife had a different kind of spirit, she could have ruined me. Even worse, she could have stopped me from being present in my kids' lives the way I want to be. I had left myself completely exposed.

But even though I was a total idiot, she stuck with me.

If I'm being 100 percent honest, I didn't start feeling completely secure with myself as a person until I finally started doing right by my wife. When I was finally able to say, "I don't need the attention of other women to make me feel whole." When I realized that I could sleep with a million different women and it wouldn't make me a man. Only being a man for my family could do that.

As I'm writing this, I'm forty-five years old. A husband and father of four.

For the first time in my life, I feel completely secure. Fully in control. Nobody can tell me anymore I'm not who I say I am. And that makes me feel great. Makes me feel whole.

To any men reading this, especially young men who are new to a marriage or a serious relationship, I want to give you a teachable moment here. If you picked up this book because you've been inspired by my success, or how I've built my career, understand that nothing I have today would be here if I hadn't stopped taking my family for granted.

I've come up in every way—professionally, physically, spiritually, and emotionally—since I stopped running around. My family is the bedrock my life is built on. A life that would have crumbled if I hadn't told my ego to shut up and corrected myself.

This is why you must always work to build up what therapist, and my friend, Elliott Connie calls "ego strength."

According to Elliott, ego strength is like muscle strength. You have to work on it consistently. If you want to start working out, you don't just walk into the gym one day and immediately bench press 185 pounds, or do twenty-five pull-ups. If you try that, you'll get frustrated and quit. It has to become a consistent part of your lifestyle.

Maintaining your "ego muscle" works the same way. You can't just wake up and say, "That's it, I'm not listening to my ego anymore." That's not going to work. Your ego is too powerful to go away the first time you push back against it.

Just like your physical muscles, building up your ego muscle has to become a consistent part of your lifestyle.

So how do you do it?

You must do it very loudly and very firmly: tell your ego that you're fine being *uncomfortable*.

Remember, your ego is an instigator. A bully. A voice that is always going to try to push you toward action, even when none is needed. And nothing triggers that voice more than the sense of being uncomfortable.

Let's say you're at a party where you don't know anyone. Everyone else seems to be friends and engaged in great conversation. You're sitting there by yourself, struggling to fit in. That's going to make you a little uncomfortable. A little unsure of yourself. As soon as that little bit of doubt presents itself, that's when your ego will pounce. "Man, these people think they're better than you," your ego might say. "They don't respect you. You need to show them."

If you listen to your ego, that's when you start overcompensating for your discomfort. You might start talking too loud. Buying drinks you can't afford. Being obnoxious. Even starting fights.

When your ego starts gassing you up that way, push back. Tell it,

"I'm fine being a little uncomfortable for a few minutes. I'll start up a conversation eventually." And you will. Even if you sit there by yourself for fifteen minutes, eventually someone will come over and start a conversation. If you're talking from a place of comfort and security, instead of panic and insecurity, it'll be a good conversation too. Which will lead to another. Soon all that discomfort that your ego was telling you was going to be impossible to overcome will actually just peacefully drift away.

Or you might feel uncomfortable in a professional setting. Especially if you're starting a new job, or working around new people. You might feel like maybe you don't belong, or aren't as exprienced as your coworkers. So in a meeting you try to make up for it by talking over people. Or loudly complaining about how stupid your boss is. You might not even really feel that way, but you've let your ego take over the conversation to ease that discomfort. To fit in. You're overcompensating for feeling out of your depth.

In a moment like that, flex your ego muscle. Let your ego know that it's normal to feel uncomfortable in a new professional setting. You don't need to remind everyone how smart you are, or how stupid other folks are. Just be comfortable and stay focused on your work. If you do that, eventually people are going to recognize your talent and dedication. Don't let your ego overpower your actual skills.

Looking back, my most ego-driven moments have all been rooted in insecurity.

When I was acting like an ass back in 2015, it wasn't because I believed that I was a star who deserved all the accolades, perks, and attention that were coming my way.

No, deep down the problem was that I *wasn't* sure. I didn't truly believe I deserved any of that. I was terrified that one day I would wake up and it would all be gone. That I'd be back on the unemployment line. Back sleeping in my childhood bedroom at my momma's house.

I couldn't deal with those anxieties, so I covered them up with fake cockiness. With arrogance. With trying to seem cool.

I'm still anxious, but now I know to tell my ego, "Relax, you're not needed here. I've got this."

I know that the anxiety isn't going anywhere, but it doesn't have to disrupt me. I've learned to be comfortable being uncomfortable.

Whenever you start to feel uncomfortable in a situation and you feel like you have to "respond," ask yourself where that urge is coming from. Do you really have to do anything when you don't know anyone at a party? Is it so terrible to sit by yourself for a few minutes at a party? Is it really that terrible to not say something on a Zoom call? Or to realize you've underdressed for an event?

Yes, those are uncomfortable moments, but all you have to do is take a deep breath and accept that you're going to make it through them.

Let's discuss. . . .

CHAPTER 20

Headlines

As an eighties baby, this is hard for me to say . . . but the first step in getting past the small talk and getting into the truth is to stop reading headlines.

Growing up, headlines were where the truth lived. Whether it was in newspapers or magazines, headlines were your introduction to what was really happening out there in the world.

Sure, there would be those sensationalist tabloid papers like the *National Enquirer* or *Star* magazine that you'd look at while waiting to check out at the grocery store. They'd have headlines like "I Was Big Foot's Love Slave" or "Bat Child Found in Cave." You knew they were only there to entertain (OK, I did use to wonder if there were some truth to the Big Foot stories.). But if you saw something written in big letters across the front of the *New York Times*, or *USA Today*, you believed that there was real reporting and research behind what was said.

Back then, if you were a reporter, and you used a lie about a story, or even intentionally mislead people, man, your career was over. Your reputation was ruined. You'd never work again.

Today, all that quality control is a thing of the past. Even though they might be written in the biggest fonts, headlines have really become the smallest of small talk. I don't know if it's the editors or the reporters who

144 Get Honest or Die Lying

write these things, but these days headlines seem to have very little relation to the stories they're promoting, let alone the actual truth.

Think I'm lying? Let me give you an example of a situation I'm dealing with right now as I'm writing this book.

If you're a fan or follower of mine, then you know that I've given the rapper known as Drake hell since he first came on the scene. It started maybe fifteen years ago, when I realized there was something about him that I just had to make jokes about. I'd call him a "thumb with eyebrows." Or I said, "There are three sexual orientations out there: gay, straight, and Drake." Yes, I was hating on him. But at the time, it all seemed hilarious.

At least to me.

You ever wonder how I ended up in Drake's now legendary diss record to Meek Mill titled "Back to Back"? What happened was people really thought I hated Drake and wanted to ruin his career. Which is far from the truth.

There were a lot of folks in the industry who wanted to destroy Aubrey Graham, as this story will bear out, but I wasn't one of them.

All the drama started one night on Twitter when Meek Mill accused Drake of having a ghostwriter. In hip-hop that is a very serious accusation, so that sent social media into a frenzy. The very next day I started getting phone calls that I would be receiving some of the reference tracks written for Aubrey Graham. The tracks, I was told, would prove that Drake used a ghostwriter.

The reason I was supposed to get the tracks was because they thought once I'd heard them, I'd go on the air the next day and start clowning Drake. I'd call him a phony and a fraud. But honestly, I didn't care that much.

I was just coming off a bad experience with Floyd Mayweather where I'd clowned his attempt to read some promos he'd recorded for iHeart Radio. Floyd had really struggled with reading the scripts and even though EVERY SINGLE PERSON on my team told me not to play the recordings on-air, I went ahead and aired them anyway.

I immediately regretted it. A lot of listeners said the audio was triggering because it brought them back to when they were being called on in school to read and were nervous. Plus, he'd tried to do iHeart a favor by reading those promos and I'd clowned him for his troubles.

The whole thing made me feel terrible and ate at my conscience.

So when I was leaked those Drake reference tracks, I felt conflicted about whether I wanted to create another media firestorm just for the sake of watching it burn.

As I often did when I was conflicted, I called up my great friend Jas Fly for advice. After I told Jas about the reference tracks, she told me that she was also friends with Drake (which I hadn't known) and wanted to give him a heads-up that I had the tracks. I told her that was fine, and she reported back that Drake couldn't believe that not only did I have the tracks, but I wasn't looking to clown him over them. Jas added that Drake appreciated my restraint, and she had even told him she had no doubt the two of us would be friends if we ever got the chance to speak. That's what led to Drake mentioning me in "Back to Back" and infamously sending me several bottles of champagne with the note, "Let's be friends."

Since then, we've been on relatively good terms. I've taken a few jabs at him, but I don't have any real beef with the guy. I just like to keep him on his toes when it comes to his music.

Which brings me to the point I wanted to raise about headlines. In 2023 Drake released a track with SZA called "Slime You Out." Those two are a combination that should set the world on fire, but the song barely created a spark when it dropped. There was a certain energy missing from it and I wasn't the only one who felt that way. So when I went on *The Brilliant Idiots*, I decided to comment on the situation. "What scares me—and it's not a scare because Drake's gonna be fine—Drake put out a song last Friday and nobody cared," I declared. "It came out last Friday, and people just started talking about the lyrics [the next week]."

Hardly the worst thing I've ever said about an artist. But Drake wasn't having it and went on IG to air his grievances.

"Are you ok Lenard??" he posted. "You kinda weirding me out G. Like you really obsessed with me or something for years like you look in the mirror and wish you saw my reflection type s--t." Drake continued his onslaught by calling me an "off-brand Morris Chestnut" and a "fucking goof." He added: "Whatever you gotta do to let it out I'm sure your 435 loyal fans will stand by you ya fuking goof."

OK, he got a few good shots in at me. The "off-brand Morris Chestnut" line was good, but in my defense Morris himself said while making an appearance on *The Jennifer Hudson Show* that he's been confused for me before, so I must not be *that* far off-brand.

Still, people wanted to hear my reaction. So when I went on *The Breakfast Club* following his posts, this is what I told folks.

"You're not gonna believe me because I'm lying," I said. "But Drake and I plan this out every time he drops an album. I'm part of the album rollout. He drops a record. I critique it. That brings more attention to the record, more attention to the project. I keep telling Drake he doesn't need me to do that. He's Drake. But for whatever reason, he wants me to do it, so I oblige."

Now, how did I start off that statement? By saying I'm lying. So why would you take anything I said after that as the truth? I don't know, but that's exactly how almost every hip-hop site framed their headlines. Here's just a small sampling:

Complex: *Charlamagne Tha God Says His Beef with Drake Is Planned*
Yahoo!: *Charlamagne Tha God Claims He's Part of Drake's All the Dogs Roll Out*

Hip-Hop DX: *Charlamagne Tha God Comes Clean About Drake Feud: "I'm Part of the Album Rollout"*

Now, why would they frame the story that way when I clearly said that I was lying?

Well, it's simple: Why lead with the truth when the lie is more entertaining?

The truth, in this case, wasn't even that exciting. I didn't like Drake's new song.

The lie, that me and Drake stay up at night hatching covert marketing plans, was much juicer. That promised to get many more clicks.

I wish I could say it was an isolated incident, but you know it's not.

A few months earlier, Andrew Schulz and I were on *The Brilliant Idiots* debating who was more popular, Taylor Swift or Beyoncé. Andrew was claiming Taylor was bigger because she had just shut down a New Jersey restaurant with her mere presence, drawing the police to the scene to control the hundreds of Swifties who'd got word of her arrival via social media. So I decided to have some fun.

"Beyoncé can't even go to restaurants," I claimed. "She's forbidden from eating at restaurants. It's actually called the Michael Jackson Law. Now you know how Michael Jackson couldn't just walk around because it caused hysteria? She'll get locked up for inciting riots. It was ten years ago they put her on that."

"Really?" asked my naive producer, Taylor. "Yeaaaaaah," I responded with all the sincerity I could muster.

It might have worked on Taylor, but Andrew knew what I was up to. He immediately launched into a story about how Beyoncé used to take lessons at his mother's dance studio in Manhattan (to be fair, his mother really did run a studio).

"Did my mother teach her how to dance? Yes," Andrew said. "My parents were instrumental in her dancing greatness. That's something that you can look up. It's closed now, but before it closed, we made sure we bestowed dancing wisdom on one of the greatest entertainers of all time."

Now, that was a bridge too far, even for me. If you've ever seen Andrew dance, you know there's no way anyone who shared the same bloodlines could ever teach Beyoncé the first thing about moving her feet. So I cut in.

"Me and Andrew just told two lies back to back."

Andrew started cracking up.

"We just told two convincing lies back to back," I repeated. "Watch, someone's going to take that clip and post it."

Well, call me Negrodomus.

The next day the internet was filled with headlines like "Charlamagne Tha God Alleges a Michael Jackson Restaurant Law Exists to Stop Celebs from Dining Out" and "Beyoncé Is Forbidden to Go to Restaurants."

The story got so big that the great Houston hip-hop legend Bun B felt the need to extend an open invitation to Beyoncé for her, in violation of the "law," to come and dine at one of his Trill Burger restaurants.

"Sorry @cthagod but the Queen @beyonce is more than welcome to dine @trillburgers" he wrote. "And we can anticipate and handle any and all issues on site bro!"

All of that, despite me CLEARLY stating in the podcast that I had made that entire story up.

Now were there bits of truth in all these stories? Sure there were.

I do believe that Drake likes picking little fights when it's time for a new album to drop. He knows that people flock to conversations like that and it will raise awareness about his project.

Just like I'm sure both Taylor Swift and Beyoncé have shut down plenty of restaurants in their day. But there is certainly no law on the books about them, or any other celeb, not being able to dine out because of their popularity.

So what can we take from all this?

Firstly, I definitely need to stop making stuff up (even though it can be a lot of fun).

Secondly, we really can't believe any of the headlines we see nowadays.

No matter what you read, no matter how trusted the source, you must pop the hood and check out the rest of the story.

If you just go off the headline, you're more than likely going to be misinformed. You owe it to yourself to find out more.

And if you don't care to do that then you don't really care about the story you're talking about, you just care about the attention you receive from talking about said story.

Let's discuss. . . .

CHAPTER 21

The Point!

One of the worst forms of small talk is when someone wants something from you.

I'm begging you—if you want something, whether it's a job, advice, a date, or money, please get straight to the point. Beating around the bush with small talk is only going to take you further from what you want.

Personally, I love it when people are direct with me. It clears up so much confusion and puts me at ease.

Recently I was at the airport after a long international flight. As I was waiting for my bags, I noticed a guy staring at me. I understand I'm at the level of notoriety where people often either know exactly who I am or think they know me but are having trouble putting a name on it. Is that Morris Chestnut? Nah, is that Tyrese? Oh, that's definitely Morris Chestnut. (And to the person reading this and thinking, "Isn't this book about honesty?," please remember what I just told you about Morris and me.)

I don't mind the stares because I'm comfortable with people coming up to me for selfies, or just to give me a pound. I'm incredibly appreciative to anyone who supports me with their time or money, and I always want to spend a moment with them.

But I'm also the guy who's gotten attacked twice in the streets of NYC. If you've ever been punched in the back of the head unexpectedly, then you know the trauma from that never really goes away. You constantly have your head on a swivel, and certain environments and situations trigger that. There's always a little voice in my head questioning what someone's true intention is when I see them approaching.

In the airport, I could tell the guy wanted to speak with me. Sure enough he started walking my way. As he approached, I could see he was struggling with something. He looked nervous. Uneasy. I started to get tense. Is this guy about to try me at the airport?

As soon as he got up to me, the first words out of his mouth were "Charlamagne, I have a speech impediment, so bear with me."

The second he said those words, all my tension deflated. I knew he wasn't going to swing on me. Wasn't going to press me on something I didn't want to talk about. He just wanted to say hi, and it was going to be hard for him to even get that out. I respected the hell out of that guy for getting straight to the point the way he did.

Getting to the point is helpful in social situations, but it's absolutely critical in professional conversations. Especially, as I said, when you're asking for something.

I've noticed that younger generations have a hard time articulating their "asks." Often they don't actually know what they want. I can't tell you how many times someone has asked me for help in the most non-specific ways possible. Especially when it comes to me helping them find work or build a relationship with someone who they believe can help them in their careers.

Their "ask" nowadays usually sounds something like this: "You need to put me on with a podcast deal." Sometimes they even have a specific person in mind: "You need to put me on with 50 Cent!!!"

What does "put me on" even mean? Does it mean you want a job? If so, what kind of job? I don't even know what you want to do!!! Be a bodyguard? A stylist? An accountant? A blunt roller? What do you want to do for that person?

And then try to imagine how that conversation would go on my end with the celebrity. "Hey, there's this guy I kinda know. I'm not sure what he does, or wants to do for you. But he asked me to reach out to you, so can you put him on?"

Doesn't that sound stupid? As if successful people have open spots on their roster just waiting to be filled with people with unknown qualifications. Why would you ever expect a successful person to just "put you on"? If that's your "plan," you're never going to make it.

Now, if I have watched you practice and perfect your craft over the years, and then heard someone had a need for the skill set you possess, then that's a different story. I would try, without even being prompted, to put your name into the mix.

In fact, I do that all of the time. I love connecting talented people not just to myself but with my friends and associates when they need help. Nothing makes me happier. To put it in basketball terms, I'm much more excited about getting an assist than I am scoring on my own. Nothing makes me feel better than helping someone improve their situation.

But simply saying, "Yo, put this guy on"? That's never going to happen. Successful people don't make it to the top by putting people "on." Especially people that they don't even know. They make it to the top by surrounding themselves with smart, hardworking people who have specific skills that move the entire team forward.

The other trait a lot of successful people share is they are very direct and specific when they are looking for something. They know how to articulate their asks so that when you finish a conversation with them, you're very clear about what they want and how they're prepared to get it.

Contrast that with a young lady who has become a mentee of mine, or as I call them, one of my "nieces." This niece shall remain nameless, but I can see her talent and work ethic, so I try to help keep her career moving in the right direction. The other day we were texting about a news story, and

I was discussing how people often confuse their emotions for facts on social media. I said, "Social Media truly has conditioned folks to think their feelings are facts. Comprehension is a thing of the past, nobody truly does any research anymore. They get online and wait to see what the general consensus about something is and then they repeat that."

That opened the door for her to vent. She said that as a journalist, she felt the bigger problem was that people don't respect journalism anymore. She said we don't put credible journalists in positions to really fly. People would rather give shows and placements to BBL girls, former athletes, celebrity baby mamas, etc. She said we can't do that and then be surprised that misinformation gets promoted. All valid points, but I hadn't seen her flex her journalism skills before, so I asked why she described herself that way. This is what she wrote back to me:

I'm not currently practicing journalism. If I'm being real with you, I'm currently trying to figure out where I fall in the mix. This is why I asked if we could have more mentor-mentee time. It doesn't involve us debating, because I am trying to find my place in this entertainment space. So with this being said, can I work for you? Or at the very least, can I send pitches to one of your platforms, be it Black Effect or Reason Choice Media. The people you touch, turn to gold. It's my turn, Unc. I'm talented and smart, but I'm not perfect, and I know with more guidance and opportunities, I'll find my place and be another one of your success stories.

From my perspective, that entire conversation was really about two questions:

Can I work for you? Or at the very least,
can I send pitches to one of your platforms?

That was her "ask." Though it had started as an interesting debate, it had essentially been small talk. She was just trying to set up that ask.

I'll give her credit, she got to the point quicker than a lot of folks would have (which she always does). But it still wasn't necessary. I'd already told her I thought she was super talented and had a great work ethic. She could have gotten to the ask even quicker, especially since she has direct access to me.

But I want to give her credit on one point: asking if it's OK to pitch an idea is a great way to put yourself in a stronger position. Even if the pitches aren't all winners at first, just the act of putting something down on paper and submitting it shows you have a solid work ethic and follow up on things. Plus, it's a way for a boss to keep track of someone they think has potential without having to make a commitment right away.

I know "pitching" isn't something that works in every industry— you can't "pitch" a school where you want to teach, or "pitch" a restaurant where you'd like to work in the kitchen—but there are things you can do to show you have a combination of talent and follow-through. Drop off a meal you made, or a cake you baked, once every couple weeks at that restaurant. Even if it reveals your skills still need a little sharpening, it'll show you're serious. Successful people know how to build talent. They just want to know they're not wasting their time when they start to make that investment.

There are a lot of people out there who want to make that pitch, or drop off that cake, but never end up doing it because they're nervous. Look, I'm the last person who's ever going to criticize you for being nervous or anxious. I feel that way almost every day. But I always fight through that anxiety because I'm even more stressed by the idea of not getting an idea out into the world because I'm too afraid to approach someone. That what-if will haunt me forever!! I have no problem with a no, but the what-if hanging over me because I never tried would hurt way worse.

What I've found is that when someone has a really good idea, or a truth they need to share, it's almost impossible for them to keep it inside.

Remember that clip of Ed Lover putting his hand over Tupac's mouth on *Yo! MTV Raps*, when Pac was trying to speak on his situation with the legendary director Allen Hughes? His lawyers and publicists had probably told him not to speak on it, but Pac just had to get it out!!!

The way Pac felt on *Yo! MTV Raps* is how you should feel when you have a great idea or find a subject you're truly passionate about. It should feel like you're about to burst if you keep it inside any longer.

Whenever you've got something that really needs to be shared, nothing can contain it. Not anxiety, not nervousness, not insecurity. And there's nothing you want to do more than get right to it. If you have an idea like that you need to share with me, don't start off with "How is the family? Damn, you working out? How 'bout them Cowboys?" Get outta here with all that. Instead, get right to the point!

It's an ability we have as kids but often lose over time. My eight-year-old is in a stage right now where if she's excited about something, she's going to let the entire world know. I can be reading to one of her sisters or be on the phone or talking with her mother, but if she's got something she wants to share, she will! If she's just watched a TV show or listened to a song she likes, she'll literally interrupt whatever we got going on just to tell us.

Now, I'm not telling you to do that as an adult, because that would just be rude, but I am telling you to be honest with yourself at all times and never lose that belief in what you love and want to share.

It's not ego, it's not selfishness, it's just pure enthusiasm and excitement. Kids don't worry about whether the world sees their ideas as good or bad. All they know is that they're good to them. And that's enough.

As we grow older, we have to find ways to tap back into that child-like enthusiasm. And honesty.

Don't get nervous about how your idea is received. Don't spend needless time worrying about all of the things that could go wrong when you put yourself out there. Don't think about any of that. Just create a pitch for your idea and let it fly.

Once again, I battle with anxiety every day. I'm constantly second-guessing myself. But when I have something I believe in, it transcends that anxiety. If I've been waiting for a moment to get in front of somebody who I feel could help me bring a situation to life, I'm going to walk through that door. Even if internally my palms are sweaty, knees are weak, and I'm about to throw up Mom's spaghetti.

I promise you, people can feel the energy when you believe in something. They will listen. And even if they don't agree with you at first, your energy and honesty can sway them.

I've seen it happen. I've been in rooms before a meeting where everyone from one company is aligned that they're not going to do a certain deal. Or green-light a certain pitch. Then someone walks through the door with so much enthusiasm and positive energy that suddenly all those skeptics can't remember what they were so worried about.

There's no small talk. No mumbling about the weather or who won the football game. That person can't wait to address the idea that's on the table. And after twenty minutes of impassioned, thoughtful, and honest talk, everyone else starts to see that person's vision too.

Kevin Hart is an absolute master at this. Nobody can work a room like Kevin. It's not just that he's passionate about his ideas. It's that he makes everyone feel "seen" too. By that, I mean he'll listen to people's questions and address them head-on. He'll talk with skeptics. Not in a combative way, but in a way that lets them know he's already thought about what they're saying and has found a solution.

That's why when I hear people question how did Kevin get to Hollywood and end up with a TV show and the *Soul Plane* movie when nobody out in LA knew him? Well the answer to that is easy. Have you ever seen him work a room? It's a skill that people like Kevin are born with; they cut the small talk and get right to the matter at hand, and by the time you're done listening you feel like whatever he just pitched you is something you now believe in just as deeply as he does.

It's incredible to watch and I feel fortunate to have been in rooms with him. Just to learn. To understand that when you have an idea you're truly passionate about, nothing is going to stop you from getting it out, and when you have an opportunity to seize everything you ever wanted in one moment, you will cut the small talk and completely lose yourself. Word to Mom's spaghetti.

Let's discuss. . . .

CHAPTER 22

I Hear Dead People

I've already talked about the importance of conversations between generations.

But forget about Gen X or Boomers. Now I want to speak on the ultimate cross-generational conversations:

The ones you need to have with your *ancestors*.

Ghosts, spirits, ancestors—whatever you want to call them, I know they're out there and I love communicating with them.

From the time I was a child, I've felt covered by them. Protected. Guided.

This kind of talk might sound surprising to some of you, but back in South Carolina it's actually not that unusual.

I already talked about it in my first book, *Black Privilege*, but a lot of folks I knew growing up believed in hags. These were little women, kind of like witches, who would come into your room at night and sit on your chest. You couldn't hear them coming, or feel them climbing up on you, but suddenly you'd wake up in the middle of the night with the sensation that you couldn't breathe.

That was the hags on you.

I saw other signs of the supernatural growing up. I had toys in my room that suddenly came to life. I saw flying saucers. One time I walked out of the Jehovah's Witness Hall and suddenly levitated in the air. I got so high that I could look down on the roof of the hall before I finally came back to the ground.

I especially never get tired of telling the story about the time in third grade when I actually turned into Teen Wolf during one of my lunch periods.

I loved the Michael J. Fox movie, and for weeks I'd been telling my friends that I was going to turn into Teen Wolf. During one particular lunch period I started trying to manifest the idea so hard that it started to work! I literally felt my ears going from round to pointed, just like a wolf's. All the other kids at the table saw what was happening, so they jumped up and ran away screaming. Unfortunately, that messed up my concentration and broke the spell.

But if they had just stayed calm, I probably would have fully transformed. There's no telling how far our third grade basketball team could have gone.

I told some of these stories on the Joe Rogan podcast, and he had what he considered a logical explanation.

"Memory's a strange thing; you can believe something and know something to be true when it didn't actually happen," Joe explained. "People have memories in their head that never happened. It's proven that you can talk someone into a memory."

I'm sure what Joe was describing is real, but so are my experiences. Joe's open to a lot of ideas that the mainstream might find offbeat, but maybe part of his mind is still blocked off to the idea of the supernatural and spiritual world. Stay open to that, Joe! You never know when you might levitate over a building.

We all need to, because there is so much to learn from the spirits.

Instead of viewing them as scary, or even silly, we need to embrace the role they can play in our lives as guides.

It's important to seek out areas where the presence of the spirits are strong. For me, those places can be found throughout South Carolina. Whenever I'm back home, especially along the Atlantic Ocean coastline in places like Gadsden's Wharf in Charleston or Kiawah Island, I can literally feel the energy of my ancestors who were brought to this country over that same ocean.

Gadsden's Wharf is where close to 40 percent of the Africans who were brought to this country in chains first landed. It's the home of the new International African American Museum, which is a long overdue recognition of the role the wharf has played in American history.

But honestly you don't need a museum to teach you about that site's history. If you just stand on the waterfront, close your eyes, and breathe slowly, you can actually feel the energy of the hundreds of thousands of slaves who passed through over the years. You can feel them questioning what's about to happen to them, but also their strength and determination. They're entering a new reality so far away from home, but they're going to figure out a way to survive. It's really inspiring to me to tap into that energy every time I'm in Charleston.

Often the messages from your ancestors land closer to home. A great example happened to me several months ago involving my third daughter. (For those keeping track, I now have four. And I'm officially retired from chasing a boy. I'm a Girl Dad and I love it!)

This daughter is only five at the time I'm writing this, but she already has a reputation in our family as a healer. I feel like all of my kids have been here before in some form, but with my third daughter the connection to our ancestors is very strong. She'll come over to me whenever she senses I'm a little down and just put her hand on my knee without saying a word. Exactly like my grandmother used to do when I was down around her. They obviously never met, so she's not mimicking anything she's seen in this world. She got it somewhere else.

One day I was at work when I got a text from my wife. "Hey Babe, just wanted to let you know that [third daughter's name that you hea-thens will never get in a book] just burst into tears and is saying, 'My grandma died, my grandma died.'"

My wife tried to console her, telling her that her grandma, my mother, was alive and well. She even offered to put her on the phone.

But my daughter quickly corrected her. "Not Popo," she cried. "Grandma Rosa Lee died!"

She was talking about *my* grandmother. Who died in 2006. And who she reminded me so much of.

Later, I got on the phone with her and asked what she was feel-ing. "Well, I'm just sad," she told me. "Grandma Rosa Lee died and I just miss her."

In some families, a five-year-old claiming to communicate with one of her ancestors might be cause for alarm, but not in mine. I was curious. When I got home that night, I pressed her again to describe what she'd felt.

At first she said she didn't want to talk about it, but finally she just reiterated that she missed Grandma Rosa Lee. So I explained to her that even though she had never actually met Grandmother Rosa Lee in person, she was still always going to be with her. That they had a connection. "She's in the spirit world now, but her spirit is always with you," I told her. "She's one of your guides, right? She'll always be guiding you." My daughter accepted that and finally felt better. I felt good too, because I knew from that moment on, my daughter would always feel like she had someone who loved her watching over her. That's a powerful feeling for a kid, or anyone, to have.

I was comfortable telling my daughter that because I've had conver-sations with my grandmother after she passed. She's an active ancestor. I remember one night right after she transitioned I had a vivid dream about her. She was sitting in her favorite chair, the one we found her body in after she passed. Except rather than an old woman, she appeared to me as a beautiful young woman. She had long, shiny, natural black hair. Not the wig I had always known her to wear.

She looked up at me and just casually began talking about my niece who had just been born. About what a lovely baby she was, and how she was going to go on to be a great child. When I woke up, I knew that my grandmother was watching over our family.

Embracing the energy of your ancestors can be a very powerful stabilizing force in your life. It can help you feel grounded whenever you feel like you're being tossed around on the seas of life.

This is why I don't like it when people casually say things like "I swear on my grandma," or "I put that on my dead daddy. . . ." *Especially* when they are lying! They don't realize the power they're potentially unleashing. I don't play about that at all.

In order to sit down and have conversations with the ancestors, you've got to quiet your mind. You need to meditate. You need to take a long walk in nature without any distractions. You need to hug a tree. Those are the ways you can start the dialogue.

Remember, your ancestors are not on your phone. They're not in your contacts list. There's no text thread you can hit them on. You can't like their tweets, or click on their IG lives.

To connect with them, you have to detach yourself from the noise of social media and embrace the silence you'll find in meditation.

That's where you'll find them. Once you shut off all the noise and distractions, you'll finally be able to hear the voices that are actually trying to help you.

Outside of meditation, another great way to get in touch with your ancestors is through studying your history. When you become very familiar with where your people come from, and what they went through, it becomes much easier to connect with them.

This can be particularly difficult for African-Americans, since our history and roots have been so purposely hidden from us. If you're Irish and your family moved here generations ago to escape the Irish potato famine, your family still might feel a powerful connection with Ireland.

Or your family might have been living in Texas for the last one hundred years, but you still hear stories about your great-grandmother's village back in Mexico. Even if you've never visited it, you still have a connection with that history. With that energy.

African-Americans have never had that, and I think we've suffered because of it. When the slave ships brought us over here, no one even gave us a slip of paper that said, "Hey, we snatched you from the town of Tema and you're from the Ewe tribe." Even that tiny connection to our past would have been so helpful. But they couldn't even give us that. They just said, "Get to work."

So I took a series of ancestry tests. I won't lie, I was nervous at first because I'm all too familiar with the story of Henrietta Lacks, the African-American woman who had her cancer cells harvested without her or her families' permission. Not to mention I'm one of those people who believe in conspiracy theories about them using our DNA to clone us and populate civilizations on Mars. Or the theory that they store Black people's DNA in order to use it against us in possible criminal proceedings. (Yes, these are the discussions about DNA sharing I have with my loved ones.)

Despite all those crazy theories running around in my head, I wanted to have that connection. The first test I took told me that my ancestry is largely West African. That was cool, but I already had assumed that. Almost all African-Americans who live in the Carolinas originally came from West Africa.

Then I had the late, great Chadwick Boseman (also from South Carolina) on *The Breakfast Club* in 2018. We were talking about the importance of finding the link to your ancestors. "As an African-American, you're always going to feel like until you make that connection, there's a disconnect," explained Chadwick. "So I took a DNA test."

I told him that I'd taken a DNA test, but Chadwick replied that he'd taken a more exacting one—African Ancestry—that could actually tell me what tribe and ethnic group I was from. "If you know you're Yoruba, from Nigeria," Chadwick explained, "you can pinpoint specific customs and rituals that are part of your past."

There was something very powerful in Chadwick's voice that got my attention. Later I'd learn that during the interview he was already dealing with the colon cancer that would end his life so prematurely. Was that knowledge what made him so passionate about finding out the exact connection he had with his ancestors? I have to believe that was a big part of it.

Following his advice, I took the African Ancestry test myself and found out that I'm largely the descendant of three ethnic groups: the Mende from present day Sierra Leone, the Balanta from present day Guinea-Bissau, and the Mandinka from present day Senegal.

If you look at the characteristics of those three groups, I think you can see the impact my ancestors have had on me. The Mende were known as very defiant people who fought back hard against attempts to enslave them. They were the tribe that famously took over the *Amistad* slave ship. Similarly, the Balanta were also known for being very resistant against the Portuguese colonizers who tried to govern them. The Mandinka are renowned for being storytellers. The *griot*, or elder who passes along history and information through the oral tradition, is a revered part of Mandinka culture.

Hmmm.

I'm descended from defiant storytellers. Whose traditions include spreading information through talking.

When it's framed like that, I have to believe my ancestors had a hand in guiding my path.

Sometimes I may have been conscious of their hand; other times I couldn't feel it on my shoulder. But I am confident they've been there for me all along.

This is why it's so important that you study your history. And make a real effort to connect with those ancestors. They experienced so much in their lives and have much valuable wisdom to pour into yours. Let's discuss. . . .

CHAPTER 23

Small Town, Small Talk

I used to sound like a broken record, telling anyone who listened, "I'm from Moncks Corner, South Carolina, population eight thousand."

It's not entirely accurate anymore—in the last decade a lot of folks from around the country have moved to South Carolina, so today the population is closer to fourteen thousand people.

I know, that's over a 50 percent increase since I was a kid, but trust me, it doesn't matter.

Moncks Corner is still the definition of a small town.

What makes a small town isn't the population, or square miles . . . a lot of times it's the mindset. When I was growing up, our cultural institutions were the Walmart Supercenter and the Huddle House.

Now, from Moncks Corner it's only about a forty-five-minute drive south to Charleston, which is a big city. Or at least the biggest South Carolina has to offer. Hell, nowadays it often takes me more than forty-five minutes to drive into work. Or to take one of my kids to practice.

So it's not like we were literally separated from the world. But it sure felt that way growing up.

When you're living in a small town, it's hard to see the path that can take you from where you are to where you want to go. I didn't take a bus past Madison Square Garden on the way to school every morning, see the Hollywood sign in the distance, or see a famous actor grabbing a latte from the coffee shop on the corner. There weren't any celebrity sightings (or lattes for that matter) in Moncks Corner.

But still, as a kid, I learned to dream about those things I could not see or experience personally. I dreamt about using my words to move people. I didn't know what form that might take (for a long time I thought it would be through rapping, until I learned that was a gift I wasn't blessed with), but I always felt that was my destiny.

We're all born with rich imaginations. Back in Moncks Corner I could only see the types of stars I wanted to emulate through TV, magazines, newspapers, and books. I saw the RESULTS of the work, not the stars' actual daily lives.

The issue is, your favorite movie or TikTok star can only motivate you so much. Some people have the rare ability to see what they want from afar and manifest it, but for most of us, we need those kinds of examples in our faces day-to-day.

A great example of this is the experience of my good friend Steven Furtick, who grew up in Moncks Corner around the same time as me and even went to the same high school that I did, Berkeley High.

My wife was actually in the same speech class as him at Berkeley High, and even then he had a reputation as a fantastic public speaker. It was clear that Steven, even as a teenager, was in a class of his own as an orator.

So it shouldn't come as a surprise that Steven went on to become an incredibly successful and impactful pastor. He even has his own mega church, the Elevation Church, in Charlotte, North Carolina.

I'm sure there are more than a few kids growing up in Moncks Corner today who feel that same calling, who would like to be known for their ability to move people with their words, to captivate audiences with their speaking.

Now, if they did their homework and asked around a bit, they might find out that someone like Steven had already laid a path for them. And I didn't use the word "homework" by chance, either. Yes, Steven has been blessed with incredible natural ability. But where did my wife meet him? In *speech class*. Even someone as naturally blessed as Steven still took the time to learn his craft and hone his skills. He literally did his homework when it came to captivating a crowd. That class taught him to think bigger. To take a skill and sharpen it to the point where he could use it as a powerful tool.

Of course not everyone has the way with words that Pastor Furtick has. But everyone has the ability to do their homework, right?

Unfortunately, not everyone does, especially when they're in a small town.

In a small town, often it can feel easier *not* to try.

When you're in a small town and you don't have a particular skill set that stands out—if you're not rushing for a hundred yards every high school football game, or the editor in the school newspaper, or writing rhymes that all your friends love—it can be easy to give up before you even really get started.

You can go with the flow in high school, but when it's time for college, that's when most folks run out of runway. You see, the attitude toward higher learning is much different in small towns versus the bigger cities and their suburbs.

In the type of schools my kids go too now, you don't have to have displayed some sort of super skill to go to college. Sure, you'll need great grades, a high SAT score, and plenty of extracurricular activities if you want to claw your way into the Ivy Leagues, but the simple act of *going* is expected at any school. My oldest daughter sees college as a place where you can figure out what your skill is. And then begin to sharpen it.

In small-town America, if you don't display that special skill by the time you're a senior in high school, it's too easy to fall through the cracks because you're not encouraged to make college a priority. *What for?* Unless you can afford it (and not many people, even in big city circles, can afford the $70k a year it takes to pay for a year at university these days), it makes more sense to just get a job.

The one exception to this scenario is trade schools. I think trade schools—where you can learn skills like automotive technology, plumbing, welding, nursing, HVAC, dental hygiene, and computer IT—are a FANTASTIC alternative. Most trade schools cost around $10k a year. And you're all but guaranteed a good paying job coming out of one. A liberal arts college costs on average $70k a year, and the only thing you're guaranteed coming out is a lot of debt. Folks are always going to need their cars fixed, pipes laid (pause), and teeth cleaned. But newspaper reporters, English professors, and even attorneys? Good luck paying off those loans.

But I digress. Let's not talk about the small-town folks who get those solid jobs. I want to talk about the folks who don't have the supreme skill from a college education or the common sense to get a job that's always going to be there for them.

I'm talking about the folks who don't go off to college, but then spend the next five to ten years drifting. Maybe hold down a shift at Walmart for a while. Then DoorDash. Maybe some bartending at Applebee's after that. Then to another job walking the aisles at Target.

The whole time, they never set their sights beyond the confines of their small town.

They stay in that small town because of COMFORT. Even if you're not moving toward your dreams, even if you wake up frustrated by your situation every day, you still don't want to move outside of your comfort zone.

You're comforted, even as you drive around dropping off Chipotle orders, that you're passing by your old elementary school playground. You're comforted knowing that when you go into Applebee's, you're going to see the same folks you used to see at Friday night football games. You're comforted knowing that everyone around you has had an almost identical experience to yours.

The thought of leaving that comfort zone is terrifying. The thought of going somewhere without those shared experiences, without those familiar faces, without those roads you've driven so many times, absolutely paralyzes you with fear.

Well, guess what. You know what's actually scarier than seeking out opportunities in the nearest city where everyone is a stranger? Where you don't see anything familiar? Where everyone else is moving at a pace that feels different to yours?

Staying in your comfort zone! That's actually the scariest thing you can do.

Trust me, it will be downright terrifying to hit that big four-oh and realize that you never took a chance. Never pushed yourself.

The worst question you can ever ask yourself is "What if?"

What if I had tried to carve out a life for myself somewhere else?

What if I had allowed myself to dream bigger?

What if I had allowed myself to become uncomfortable?

What if I had purposely challenged myself and everything I ever believed?

Those are the questions that will keep you up at night. Questions that are scarier than any episode of *American Horror Story* or *The Walking Dead*.

One of the keys to my own evolution was being able to ask myself those questions in high school, before it was too late. I only had to make mistakes once before I knew I wanted something better.

I said to myself, "Whatever everyone else is doing in Moncks Corner, I'm going to do the opposite." If everyone was drinking and smoking weed after school, then guess who was going home and reading? If everyone was selling dope, guess who tried to get an honest job?

Me.

And guess what? Choosing another path made people mad.

They didn't like that I disconnected. They said, "What, you think you're better than us?"

My response in my mind was "Of course not, I just want better."

That might sound harsh, but there is absolutely nothing wrong with wanting to better your life and better your circumstances.

If wanting that for yourself makes people feel uncomfortable, then that's on them. You should never feel like you have to apologize for wanting more for your life.

I show everyone love, I show everyone respect, and I try to share my blessings with as many people as possible.

But if some of those blessings came from me making better choices than you, then sorry buddy. It's time for you to look in the mirror. Not at me.

It's amazing to me that when it comes to sports, acting, rapping, or business, we love to say who's better. We love to debate who is the "GOAT."

But when it comes to our own environments, to our own backyards, wanting to be better (let alone "the best") suddenly becomes a negative. We love to hear someone brag about their bars and dunking on someone, but hearing someone bragging about their degrees, investment account, and the hours they put in at the job isn't cool for some reason.

You can never let that mentality impact you. Your job is not to keep other people comfortable with their choices. Your job is to make choices that are going to help you get where you want to, without hurting anyone else in the process.

One of my favorite quotes is from William Jennings Bryan: "Destiny is not a matter of chance, it's a matter of choice."

I do not believe the destiny of anyone reading this book is to live a life of small talk. Of small thoughts. Of small ambitions.

When you think small, you end up hating on the people you grew up with that advance past you. Trust me, that type of hate causes a particularly potent brand of venom. A venom so strong that it will poison you—from the inside—too.

Avoid that sort of pain. Don't be upset at a person who was able to evolve and grow past whatever small-ass box y'all grew up in. Don't be jealous of individuals who had the balls to do what you were afraid to do. Especially when they are people from your small town who took those big steps you were afraid to take. Follow in their path. You won't regret it.

Namaste.

Let's discuss. . . .

CHAPTER 24

The Gossip Files

It's almost impossible not to gossip. Think about it: you walk around with a device in your hand at nearly all times that gives you a direct line to the news cycle, which is nowadays filled with more gossip—he said this, she did that—than anything resembling real news.

Now, when I say real news, what I mean is hardcore information. Something that, when you read, watch, or listen to it, feels weighty and substantial. You come away from consuming that news like, "Yeah, I just learned something valuable." Next thing you know, you're at a party with some friends like, "Oh did you know about such and such?" (Pro tip: if you can read or listen to something daily that makes you sound smarter at parties, then you're on the right path.)

But that's not really what I'm talking about here. Because real news is increasingly difficult to find. Instead, what we have is gossip blogs and gossip bloggers. Used to be that they would publish things on actual websites, but in the days of podcasts, TikTok, and YouTube, it's more common that it's just some people getting on these apps and popping off at the mouth about what some "celebrity" got caught doing last night.

I put "celebrity" in quotes because I don't know what a celebrity is these days. Historically, you had to have actually accomplished something to be celebrated. Military leaders became famous for winning battles; painters and sculptors made majestic works that now sit in museums across the world; writers wrote novels, poems, and plays that were read by the masses; musicians made records that people bought and sang in front of crowds who paid money to see them; and movie stars acted in films that actually made hundreds of millions at the box office.

Nowadays, it's the complete opposite. We have an entire generation of people who are famous only for being famous. They're famous for absolutely nothing. I'm reminded of this every day when I look at Instagram and discover a new "influencer." They'll have six million followers. That's bigger than the population of some major US cities. But when I try to deduce what it is they actually do, I realize that what I'm actually looking at *is* what they do. They post pictures on Instagram. They do dances on TikTok. And now they're famous.

Is that a celebrity? Not to me. But maybe I just see things differently.

And yet these are the people the blogs obsess over. They dial into their social media–generated drama, report on it—hey, these people are famous, right?—and in turn convince innocent folks to get all worked up and invested in those lives. Now here you are wasting your time focusing on some cooked-up narrative that ain't really contributing much to your well-being, and it's all because we've placed some outsized level of importance on people who, at the end of the day, really ain't doing shit.

You know how I know these narratives are cooked up? Because I, myself, have been on the receiving end of so much gossip over the years. When I see that stuff, I'm like, *Wait, what? They're saying I did what?* Now, I'm pretty sure if I had done that thing, I'd remember it. But these folks are so convincing, they'll have you questioning yourself. Like "Shit, maybe I really did do that."

That's one of the most interesting things about the truth. Even when you know for damn sure you didn't do something, gossip is so powerful that it will have you thinking you did. The truth is no match for a bunch of people talking about you on the internet (or in real life).

And as we know from many of the instances of online bullying that people (both famous and not famous) go through, it can have disastrous effects on your mental health. Depression, anxiety—and as we saw when the CEOs of Meta, X, Discord, TikTok, and Snap testified before the Senate on child exploitation, some kids have even killed themselves over things that were said about them online.

That's why I have a hard-and-fast rule: don't message me anywhere—text, Instagram, carrier pigeon, old school snail mail—about anything anyone has ever said about me on a podcast, in a YouTube video, or in a tweet. I repeat, do not share it with me.

I am not going to engage!

What other people say about me is none of my business. That's their opinion. Last time I checked, I was still breathing, so I know the facts about my life. All that he said, she said—that doesn't resonate with me, because I was there. There is no disputing the truth if you have lived it.

And how come people rarely call to tell you when someone says something good about you? Meanwhile, they have no problem giving you the negative. Then they act surprised when you tell them you have no idea what they're talking about. "You didn't hear what such and such said?" "No. Fuck no. Why would I hear that?"

One time, a friend was shocked when I told them I hadn't heard what someone supposedly had said about me on a podcast. I'm like—why would I have heard that? I was actually on vacation at the time, actively trying to disconnect from the world for a week or two. Why would I be seeking out news about myself? I know where I'm at. I was only answering the message because I made the mistake of pulling my phone out on vacation, and this is what I have to deal with—gossip! This is exactly the kind of small talk a vacation is meant to get you away from.

I know it's hypocritical to hear me say I don't like gossip. On *The Breakfast Club*, we have "Jess with the Mess" with my good sister Jess Hilarious.

Here's the reality: WE ALL *LOVE* GOSSIP. It's fun to gossip.

But what I want to challenge you to do here, and myself as well, is to keep away from gossip on the important issues. To seek out real sources of information, as opposed to simple commentary, on the topics that really impact our lives. If messytea034978504329 on X wants to gossip about what rapper is hooking up with what other rapper, or who got what plastic surgery, that's not important. Who cares? And if you're listening to some TikTok influencer about real issues, talking about what kinds of people you should hate or who deserves to live in your country or what's going to happen with the economy—you're wasting your time. Access to gossip isn't the same as expertise on important life topics. We desperately need to improve our collective media literacy. As much as this is about small talk, what it's really about is your ability to navigate what you consume.

The key is demanding more from the information you engage with. I can tell you what the problem is, I can even give you some strategies to avoid the problem, but as with all things related to self-improvement, we often forget that the most important part of the equation is the "self." I can't do it for you; you have to do it.

As I said, gossip is something we have an appetite for. And it's a symptom of human nature. From probably the minute people could talk, they started gossiping. Look at the ancient Greek myths—they're filled with gossip. Same thing for the Christian Bible. Filled with folks talking behind each other's back. I don't know much about other religious scriptures, but I wouldn't be shocked if they had some gossip in them too. It's part of every culture, every society.

That's fair, but we need to elevate the conversation around gossip. You can do this by simply looking at anything in the news cycle and asking yourself, "What is this story really about?" By going deeper than the headlines, you can discover the root issue.

Here, let's try it together. This is a headline from a website called Pitchfork: "Kanye West Kidnaps and Buries Pete Davidson amid Roses in Animated New 'Eazy' Video."

I can look at that headline and see, in two seconds, what it's really about. It's not about a video. It's about Kanye bullying Pete Davidson for the same reasons that have fueled a lot of his actions over the years: if you don't deal with your trauma, your trauma will ultimately deal with you. Hurt people will hurt people. And when your trauma is unhealed, as it is in Kanye's case, you will self-destruct.

That should be your takeaway from an article like that. Not whatever nonsense happened in the video.

Another example: A while back the actress Keke Palmer got caught dancing on Usher at his residency in Vegas. She had on a sexy outfit. Her baby daddy was not feeling it; he left a comment on Twitter about her dressing too provokingly while being a mother.

Pretty quickly, this whole thing became a trending topic. Her husband was getting slandered. People were calling him insecure. They wished horrible things on this young man. It was sad.

Now, this, in a nutshell, was gossip personified.

The larger issues were simple to see, and nobody had to send him these hateful-ass messages. It's true, Keke hurt her man's feelings. But it was also an opportunity to have a conversation about how mothers and wives and girlfriends have the right to still be sexy. Just because you're a mom doesn't mean you can't be feeling yourself.

We could also just chalk it up to Keke and Usher being entertainers. Just because you do something on stage, doesn't mean it's who you are. That's a persona, the person you want people to think you are. But that's not really who you are.

Take it from me, during my days as a shock jock I played the role of Super Horny Man. I was inappropriate to damn near every female guest that came in the studio. I could tell you with a straight face that it was all entertainment, because it was.

But try telling that to my wife. She did not accept that that's what I had to do, and she wanted no part of it.

Now, think about if that was Usher, the guy who once sang, "Don't leave your girl round me, true player for real ask my nigga Pharrell." He's been telling us for two decades, "DON'T LEAVE YOUR GIRL AROUND ME!!!" Well shit, imagine if it was your girl who got left around him. You'd be mad as hell, too.

Side note: Usher on stage is a persona, but that persona still has real impact. Usher the persona needs to pay for his crimes against mankind. And by mankind I mean all the happy homes ruined during his residency in Vegas. Usher (persona!) was out here recklessly serenading people's significant others every night—he couldn't ask, "Where all the *single* ladies in the house tonight?" Give us a break, Usher. Instead, he was just singing to anyone and everyone. That man knows his power. Be real.

I've seen it up close and personal: that domestic terrorist named Usher serenaded my wife at one of his shows, didn't just serenade her, brought her a dozen roses. And I really wish that when he tried that with my wife, I grabbed his hand, so he would have been singing to the both of us. I should have jumped right in the middle of all that, grabbed his hand, and demanded he sing to me as well. In fact, my wife can hold your right hand, and I'll hold your left hand and you can sing "My Boo" to the both of us. See, now we having a larger conversation about teamwork!!!

Let's discuss. . . .

CHAPTER 25

Time 4 Sum Aksion

I don't care what word you use to describe your political affiliation, what religion you worship, or what philosophy you subscribe to. Your ideology, beliefs, principles—none of those things matter more than your *actions*.

To show you just how deeply I believe in this truth, I want to invite you into a place that I usually keep *extremely* off-limits: my group chat.

It was a couple of months ago when the following question popped up on my phone:

"Would y'all mess with someone who worships Satan?"

Again, this was in a group chat, so maybe my friend was just trying to stir the pot (after all, what else is a group chat good for besides stirring the pot and talking shit during football season?). But even if this was just a bored middle-aged man trying to be provocative, he had my attention.

"Helllll Nooooo!," I wrote back, instinctively. Yet the more I thought about it, the more I realized I was being too intentionally dismissive. I was basically being the kind of person who this entire book is telling you to get away from. So I hit the chat again:

"Who knows? It depends how their worship impacted their actions. Besides, y'all probably with some Satan worshippers right now."

Like I said, it *shouldn't matter what someone believes in*, if their actions are righteous, then I have to respect them. If you're not harming anyone, whether it's physical *or* emotional, and if you're not projecting your views onto someone else in a way that makes them uncomfortable and violates who they are and their place in the world, then my attitude is: you do you, and I'll do me. And that's OK. We can both coexist.

My buddy had a different take.

"I wouldn't be cool with anyone who worshipped Satan, I couldn't even co-exist in the same space peacefully. It would have to be a conflict."

Now, I have to be honest and give you a little context about this guy.

He is a CRIP.

To be fair, he's also a rapper (I'll leave him nameless, but he's had a solid career in music and is successful in other business endeavors). And while he's not an active gang member, I had to assume that he probably was still in touch with folks who were not exactly on the up-and-up.

It was my time to stir the pot. So I wrote back:

"Are Satan worshippers worse than murderers?"

He responded that they were. His belief was that simply *worshipping* Satan—as opposed to, say, worshipping God, as most of us do—was worse than actually taking someone else's life. To him, committing a Devilish act, one that the Bible also forbids (Exodus 20:13: "You shall not murder"), was bad, but worshipping the actual Devil was worse. When it came to ideology versus action, he was more concerned with the ideology. Go ahead, kill your brother, who cares; just don't worship Satan.

The problem with this logic is that Bible scripture tells us that if we don't do x, y, and z, then we are submitting our will to Satan—not God—so it doesn't really matter what anyone *believes*, so long as their *actions* are one with the worshipper of Satan. And let's be honest, a lot of us so-called Christians are guilty of this.

The Bible tells us to put others before ourselves. If you've ever gone to Walmart on Black Friday, you know how closely some folks are following those instructions.

The Bible tells us to forgive; well, I bet you can list five people that you're actively plotting against right now . . . or at least holding a grudge on.

The Bible tells us to keep the Sabbath day holy; but let's keep it real—Sunday is for the NFL for a lot of us, not God.

I could go on and on.

My point—when you look at actual *actions*, what's the difference between us and Satan worshippers? Are those of us who believe in God somehow better because if we do wrong (and have the self-awareness to acknowledge it), we pray to God for forgiveness? Does repenting make up for all the things we do that put us on the same level as the person who is loud about worshipping Satan?

(I do need to say one thing about Satan worshippers. Another friend of mine—not in the group chat—knows someone in the actual Church of Satan. Apparently none of them actually worship Satan, or believe in evil. They're just trying to make a point about First Amendment rights in this country and how much power Christians have. It's all a big joke that we're falling for. Not saying that's every Lover of Lucifer's opinion, just something I was told.)

Back in the group chat, I continued to press my point. I wasn't just stirring the pot anymore, I was making a good ol'-fashioned Low Country seafood boil (that's with *extra* Old Bay, for those who don't know).

"What about a person who believes in Satan, but has never broken any of the 10 Commandments. Would you still be in conflict with a person like that?"

That one sat on "read" for a minute. Clearly I had him off balance. Then the response:

"Worshipping Satan is different."

As it happens in group chats—which are basically the literal representation of small talk (short statements, in tiny letters, on a small screen, that are only looked at for a short period of time)—the conversation hit a stalemate. He wasn't really hearing me, even though I was hearing him.

My arguments were falling on deaf ears.

And then to prove that point, he followed up with the following: "Fuck Satan and his followers."

It was hard to disagree with that statement. I mean, yeah, fuck Satan. Obviously. And fuck Hitler too. And King Leopold II of Belgium while you're at it.

It was an obvious point, but I still had to acknowledge it.

"Yes Fuck Satan and his followers . . . now stop sinking."

"Sinking" was a typo, because I was typing too fast, but I followed it up with "*sinning*".

Even with those verses, I wasn't sure I was getting all the way through to him. So I decided to put it in language I knew he'd understand.

"We can't claim one set but bang for another."

And, before he could respond, another one:

"We gotta stop lying to ourselves."

Because my friend was definitely lying to himself.

You know how I know he was?

Because he never responded to that last text.

But if he had, this is what I had waiting behind the "..." bubble (hopefully he's reading this book):

"What's worse? A white supremacist who hates Black people but has never done any harm to those he's prejudiced against or a gangbanger who has actually killed Black people, including kids and elderly people in the crossfire?"

Trust me, I don't write those words lightly. I'm from the *South*. I understand that being a white supremacist in ideology alone *still* supports a violent, racist, and repressive society.

But I'd still prefer that to someone who physically and literally pulls the trigger and takes the lives of his brothers and sisters.

The other thing I would have sent him is this quote from 2 Timothy 2:26:

"Then they will come to their senses and escape from the devil's trap. For they have been held captive by him to do whatever he wants."

Basically, we can't claim one set (God) but on the low be banging for another (Satan).

Which is why I'm always amazed that so many folks, even gang-bangers—can be so judgmental of others based on their *ideology* while being so willing to overlook almost anything when it comes to people's *actions*.

I don't care what label you give yourself or what label the world gives you—Christian or Satanist, Crip or Blood—I am only going to judge you by what you *do*.

I don't put much stock in *perception*.

Now, I am not foolish enough to think that a belief, especially one like white supremacy, can't be dangerous in itself.

And yet, extreme as it is, the thinking at the root of those people's actions begins with the very thing that I am imploring you to get away from: worrying more about what someone says they believe in—their religion, their politics, and even their identity—than about whether they're living right in God's eyes (however you choose to define God, or whatever higher power you believe in, whether it's a religion or even a philosophy set, like Stoicism, to give you a moral compass).

Here on earth, we humans have no way to see through the words people throw around to portray themselves to the world. That's why I say I leave it up to the Almighty, because only He can see all.

It was the wise and the honorable Tupac Shakur who once said, "Only God can judge me."

Let's discuss. . . .

CHAPTER 26

Imposterism

For many years, I felt like I somehow didn't deserve my life. Things would be going well, but deep down, something inside was . . . *off.*

I'd read a positive article about myself, or find myself rubbing elbows with people I really admired, but there'd still be this voice in my head.

"Man, who the fuck are you? Do you really think you're as smart as people think you are? Do you really believe you're on the same level as these folks you get to break bread with? You know that you're not. The world just hasn't figured it out yet. . . ."

I think a lot of people—especially Black people, women, and people of color in general—experience this. Where you never feel you truly belong. Where you're constantly worried someone is going to figure out you're a fraud. Where no matter how good your life may seem, you're somehow not worthy of having it.

I could never name this feeling, until my therapist finally explained it to me: imposter syndrome.

Now, when I say that women and POC know this feeling, it's not just a hunch. In fact, the origin of imposter syndrome dates back to the year I was born, 1978. That was when two professors at Oberlin College, Pauline Clance and Suzanne Imes, first published their academic paper "The Imposter Phenomenon in High Achieving Women: Dynamics and Therapeutic Intervention."

They spent five years studying 150 high-achieving women. The women confessed that despite the accolades they'd attained, they still felt, deep inside, as if they were intellectually phony. These women lived in a constant state of anxiety. They believed—like me!—they were always one step away from being found out.

Over time, the theory about imposter syndrome took hold. And many people all over the world began to realize they too had experienced it.

A lot of it goes back to childhood. Since I was a kid, I had people telling me I had a big nose, that I was ugly, that I was a nerd. I didn't have much confidence in myself.

Probably most impactfully, I was molested by quite a few older people growing up. One older woman in particular definitely did a number on me. I'll hear a lot of teenage boys and even men say things like "Man, I wish an older lady had touched on me," but trust me, when it actually does happen to you, it's not as cool as you think it is. It makes you very confused. Especially, as it happened in my case, as soon as I wouldn't let the woman do it anymore she started telling me how ugly I was.

It led me to being a chronic people pleaser. Why? Because I felt like if I let people down, they would make me feel the same way I felt after that older woman called me ugly. I figured if I just did whatever folks wanted me to do, then that wouldn't happen again. That's why sexual molestation can really fuck up the mind of a child for a long time. That mind is still developing and it develops with that pain present.

Despite feeling down about myself, there were so many people who believed in me. People who saw an intelligence and talent in me that I didn't really see in myself yet. This is why it's important for adults to show kids that you care, like literally grab them by the collar and ask them, "What the hell is your problem?" "What are you doing?" "Why are you just sitting there letting all this talent go to waste?" You need people that can see what you have but also know what you need to be successful. "There's some good things going on in that head of his. He just needs a change of scenery."

An assistant principal at Berkeley High School named Sadie Brown said that about me once at a disciplinary hearing. She's the reason I didn't get expelled from Berkeley High School and got transferred to another high school, Stratford, where my mother was a teacher.

My point is that, throughout my life, there have been people who saw something in me. They saw the person who I was supposed to be.

But even with folks like Principal Brown in my corner, I still struggled to see myself the way they saw me.

They told me I was great. But in my mind, I'm like, "No you're not, you're a piece of shit!"

I deal with this even today.

One time, I was on a mental health panel with Tracie Jade Jenkins and Taraji P. Henson. I was introduced as a mental health advocate. My instant reaction was "Who, me? Absolutely not!"

Tracie turned to me and said, "My brother, whether you want to be or not, you are. You know, you're out here sharing your story in a large way. It has impacted a lot of people. So yes, you are a mental health advocate."

My imposter syndrome didn't want to let me believe it, but she was right. And I had to embrace it. I had to say, "You know what, this is going to be my life's work, this is what I really care about, I want to help people heal."

It's crazy to say this, but for me, that was a moment when things really really started to open up. That's when this imposter syndrome, this thing I had been feeling for so long, began to disappear.

Because I'd simply been sharing what I'd been through. And by me sharing those things, I'd helped inspire and influence others to go and do the same things I had done. To go and do the work. To man up, or woman up, and deal with their shit. That's what being of service does, it gives you a sense of purpose; sharing my mental health struggles was an act of service, and you will always find your true purpose in life through service to others.

And what I learned is, you can't make me feel like an imposter when all I am doing is expressing what I've gone through. It's my story!! I know we are flooded every day online with other people's opinions of us, but I KNOW ME. That's all that matters! I'm not trying to convince you about who I am.

But all the tough talk aside, it's not like you ever truly get over this shit. Not if you're growing and evolving the way you're supposed to. Because at every level, you're going to ask yourself—"Do I belong?"

Every move I've ever made in my career, I've been thinking that. Then I have to remember something my dad told me—you're never as good as they say you are, and you're never as bad as they say you are.

Sometimes this imposter syndrome stuff is simple anxiety. Pastor Sarah Jakes Roberts once told me "anxiety and fear are closely related. They're almost like cousins. Remember, fear is partially rooted in a lack of understanding. And anxiety is like that, too.

"When you're in a new environment, around new people, having a new experience, there's going to be a certain level of anxiety. Just because it's new and you don't know the terrain."

The opposite of this would be your house. When you're walking around your house, you're comfortable. You know where everything is. You know who lives there. There's no surprises, it's yours!

But if you're in the crib and hear a noise in the middle of the night, you're gonna jump your ass up out that bed real quick and probably go get your firearm if you a proud 2A representer like me, and rightfully so because you're startled! That noise is considered out of place in the comfort zone you call home.

New terrain, uncomfortable; your house, comfortable. Life is a lot like this.

As you reach new levels in your life, there's new levels of anxiety. Fear comes into play. You don't really understand what's going on. You become like that noise in the middle of the night. Something feels out of place; am I supposed to be here?

But you have to remind yourself—yes, you are. You belong.

I talk to myself like this all the time.

In the conversation I have with myself, I'm either extremely humble or super-cocky.

On the one hand, I'm humble because I'm grateful for everything. Sometimes just being in a room with someone, I feel really blessed. It could have been anyone, but it's me!

On the other hand, I'm super-cocky because that's the only way to keep that imposter syndrome in check. Am I lucky, or am I in this room because I worked for it? It couldn't have been *anyone*, it was supposed to be me!

I also KNOW God plays a role. That's been a constant in my life. I'm here because God wants me to be here. Even if I don't think I'm worthy, God knows that I'm worthy, and because He knows it, I truly am.

Otherwise, I wouldn't be here. There's a divine purpose for everything. And you're here, just like I am, because God wanted you in this position. There's something you did. Something you said. It got you here in this moment. You're not just here for no reason.

You can get lucky. Luck exists.

But you can't stumble into success.

Let's use the good brother Kevin Hart as an example. On the *Club Shay Shay* podcast, which has now been watched nearly sixty million times, Katt Williams claimed Kevin Hart was a "Hollywood plant."

By this, he was trying to say that Kevin hadn't worked for all that he'd achieved. That Kevin was an imposter.

The world sees Kevin as an incredibly funny, wildly successful comedian. But the narrative became Kevin Hart isn't really all that.

As way of proof, look at the fact Kevin got a network television sitcom before anyone really knew who he was (that would be *The Big House*, which ran for six episodes on ABC in 2004, before it got canceled).

But as I said in a previous chapter, I've seen Kevin up close. Nobody works a room like Kevin. Nobody talks to people like Kevin.

And it's not just an act. Kevin has this thing. It's what politicians, celebrities, and other great leaders all possess. He makes everyone, from the most important person in a room to the least, feel special. Speaking of politicians, I was always told Bill Clinton had that charm and I saw it firsthand for myself once. We were at an event and I was introducing the former President to my wife. It was like he started glowing. He looked down at her, looked her right in the eyes, shook her hand, said her name, asked how she was doing, and then said something that made her chuckle. "OK enough already," I told Bill Clinton. "You've been shaking her hand long enough." Bill Clinton put his hand to his mouth, like he's in deep thought for a few seconds, looked around, and said: "Charlamagne, some years ago you would be in real trouble, but I'm harmless now." I laughed. Deeply. I understood that he was just joking and I genuinely like that kind of "humor." (It instantly makes you funny and likable in my eyes and that, my friends, is key!!!)

See, some people, like a Bill Clinton or a Kevin, are the type of personalities who are so genuinely themselves that you *want* to like them. You never forget how people like them make you feel. So I can imagine Kevin in a room back then, getting in front of those executives. They might not have known who he was, but they probably really LIKED him. Because that's part of Kevin's talent. He gets people to root for him.

At the same time, I could see how Kevin's TV show might not have done well. I could see his TV show getting canceled because he was new to Hollywood, because he hadn't built up a fan base yet that would support him in those type of endeavors. He didn't cheat the process at all, he was just very early in it. Things like that happen.

You can sell yourself enough to get an opportunity, but that opportunity may not work out the way you want, because you weren't necessarily ready. That doesn't mean you're an imposter. Maybe you needed to be in that room simply to learn. An imposter isn't even getting in the room.

Another thing that makes people feel like they're imposters is social media. Pastor Steven Furtick says that "the reason we struggle with insecurity is because we compare our behind the scenes with everyone else's highlight reel."

On social media, no one shows you their progress, their mistakes, their setbacks. The blemishes of life are literally removed. Everything is carefully curated. Everything is perfect.

It's impossible to reach the standard of success that social media shows you. The vision of perfection that exists online is just that—a vision! It's unattainable.

My whole life has been a series of mistakes, with me figuring things out in order to get to where I am today. Yes, I am in the Radio Hall of Fame, but I was fired four times along the way there. And maybe they'll be a fifth out there. Who knows? My life—just like yours—has been the complete opposite of a highlight reel. There have been plenty of bumps along the road. Some straight-up crashes even.

Tyler Perry once said you have to aim for worthy. If you don't get there, God will take away whatever was bestowed on you. And only recently have I begun to feel that I am worthy.

I'll be driving and energy overcomes me. I feel really blessed. I feel grateful. Everything that I've done, everything that I'm doing, everything I'm going to do, I'm worthy of it.

It's been revelatory. It's like a drug. When it happens, I'm like, "Is this what it feels like to be on Molly?" If so, sign me the fuck up.

Worthiness fills the emptiness that lies deep inside. Without it, you can achieve greatness, but that greatness will never fill you up. The world will see you as great; but you will never feel it yourself.

But I'm not perfect. And imposter syndrome is like the Marvel Universe. Soon as you think it's dead, here comes another variant from the Multiverse.

When that happens, and I'm truly at a loss for what to do, I sit there, exploring the dark recesses of my mind, searching for answers, and ask myself: "What would DJ Khaled do?"

You may laugh at that, but I'm serious. If there was a situation I was in, where let's say I didn't feel so comfortable, if I could replace myself with DJ Khaled, how would he act, what would he say and what would he do?

DJ Khaled has to be one of the most confident, self-assured people in the world. I don't think I have ever seen DJ Khaled project that he's nervous, out of place, or feeling that he cannot do anything he wants to do. Whatever he's on, whatever his parents told him when he was a child, needs to be bottled and sold as a prescription.

Shit, if I could have a small percentage of the self-confidence that DJ Khaled has, I would believe that I belonged in any room I set foot in. That I deserve everything I've got. That I truly am the impactful voice people say I am.

Most importantly, I would get what I want. Which is what DJ Khaled is all about.

Recently DJ Khaled took a vacation to Barbados. Now, me or you go on vacation to Barbados, we're sipping rum punches by the beach.

Not DJ Khaled. He's on vacation, he's online, documenting the whole thing. But not only is he documenting it—he's *documenting it with a purpose.*

See, small talk is an Instagram Story, a TikTok, a tweet. "Check me out, I'm here, you're not here, but hey, look at me."

That "macro" talk is what DJ Khaled is doing. He's making these videos, showing the world he's in Barbados, but really, he's doing it for an audience of one. He's doing it for a girl. Not just any girl. But, to quote one of her famous songs, "the only girl in the world."

Who's he doing it for? Of course, if he's in Barbados, he's doing it for Rihanna.

"I want to breathe the same air that Rihanna breathes," he says in one video. He dubs the country "Rihados." He's going to her house, he's meeting the prime minister!

Now, Khaled's already made hits with Rihanna. You remember "Wild Thoughts." That's still ringing off.

But Khaled doesn't have imposter syndrome. He didn't just get lucky. He's not content to just get into the room. He wants to stay in the room. In other words, he wants, as he might say, "another one."

Someone with imposter syndrome, they might feel like, "Rihanna did this for me once, I'm not going to bother her again. She just had a kid, she's married now, did the Super Bowl halftime show. RiRi's leveled up. I'll leave her alone."

Not Khaled. Khaled is self-assured. He believes. If he can just link back up with Rihanna, he'll get another hit.

And you know what, he's probably right.

Khaled likes to say, WE THE BEST!!!

You can't be the best without first believing you are. And that's what DJ Khaled does. So when your imposter syndrome is acting up, just ask yourself, "What would DJ Khaled do?"

Let's discuss. . . .

CHAPTER 27

Echo

A lot of folks say they don't want "yes men" in their lives. They swear up and down that they're committed to having people in their circle who always keep it real with them.

That sounds great in theory, but in practice it's often a different story.

It's human nature to gravitate to people who tell you what you want to hear all the time. They make you feel comfortable. They make you feel validated. They make you feel safe.

But I promise you, there's no talk smaller in the world than false flattery. No talk smaller than empty enthusiasm.

In the end, harsh truths and constructive criticism that your true friends give you is going to be what allows you to make the best decisions.

Personally, I treasure those friends who don't just blow smoke up my ass. That's why I have a tight circle of well and not so well-known names that I lean on to keep it real with me. People who won't hesitate to pick up the phone and text me, "You were outta pocket today," or "Lemme tell you why you were wrong about that. . . ."

I want to make it clear this is different from the Demotivational Speaking I referred to earlier. In fact, let's call it *refined* Demotivational Speaking. Refined Demotivational Speaking isn't intended to make you quit, it's intended to make you ask, "Am I doing this for the right reasons?" Sometimes we start going down paths because we see those paths leading to success for others. That doesn't mean that's your PATH. The Refined Demotivational Speaker only says "F Your Dreams" if they're someone else's dreams.

But even when it comes to my friends telling me hard truths, I'll admit that's not always easy feedback to hear. But I've come to accept that very often the only way for a person to truly grow is to feel *small* first.

Remember that feeling you used to get as a child? After one of your parents caught you doing something you weren't supposed to. Or when you peed in your bed. Or had to hand them a report card filled with Ds and Fs.

Moments that made you feel small. Like you just wanted to dive under your covers and hide (unless you had actually peed on them).

Well, when your people truly keep it real with you, it's going to touch your inner child. It's going to bring you back to that feeling of fear and failure.

But when that happens, try to remember the energy your parents (hopefully) gave you when you messed up. They didn't scold you out of bitterness. Or out of envy. They corrected you out of love.

Try to take your friends' words the same way. Someone close to you challenging you is not an attack. It's an act of love. They're telling you how you can be better because they *want* you to be better.

Yes, for a moment that criticism is going to sting. Your inner child is going to be like, "Damn! That hurt!" But then you have to realize that you're not a child anymore. You're a grown-ass adult.

So instead of asking for a tissue to blow your nose, ask for more feedback. Because that's what you want. Honest feedback from someone who has your back.

Just the other day, I was in a hotel room with my wife, staring in one of its big, well-lit mirrors. The kind of mirrors you don't really want in your home because they're a little too honest, a little too revealing.

I was staring at myself, and all I could see was how much weight I was putting on. I'd been going to the gym religiously, and really trying to watch what I eat, but I'm a middle-aged guy. It's getting harder and harder to keep the pounds off.

So after staring at myself for a few moments, I said out loud, "Man, I really gotta lose twenty pounds! I really gotta get it together!"

My wife looked up, looked at me, looked at my reflection in the mirror, and said, "Yeah, you're fat."

Man, those three little words hit me like a ton of bricks! Never mind that I had just announced that I was fat myself, I didn't want to hear it from her. I wanted to hear, "Stop it, baby, you look great!" Or even just "Oh, I love some little love handles on my baby!"

But not, "You're fat."

The second she said that, I was that little kid again who was insecure about his appearance. Who felt like he was a little too chubby. Whose nose was a little too big. Whose thighs kinda rubbed together.

But even though it upset my inner child, my wife had told me exactly what I needed to hear at that moment. I didn't need reassurance. I didn't need babying.

No, I'd started to let myself go over the Christmas holidays and I was getting fat. I needed to hear that.

She hadn't gone out of her way to tell me, or started making little comments when my shirts were fitting too tight. But when I brought up the subject, she didn't brush it away. She told me the truth.

And hearing that hard truth gave me the determination to stop with the sweets, stop with the french fries and burgers I'd been eating over the holidays, and get back on a healthier diet.

You need voices like that in your professional life too. I remember when I was getting ready to film my TV show *God's Honest Truth* for Comedy Central. TV takes me a little bit out of my comfort zone, especially when I'm starting a new show. I get a little nervous.

God's Honest Truth, in case you never saw it, was the type of late-night show that's always filmed in front of a studio audience. But as we began prepping the first season, I got an idea in my mind: we're not going to tape in front of an audience.

I started telling the production staff, "Man, studio audiences are corny. The laughter always feels forced. We're going to tape this without anyone there."

It wasn't a great idea, but since it was my show, most people didn't push back. We taped a rehearsal without an audience, and I knew deep down it didn't feel right, but I wasn't ready to admit I was wrong. I kept telling everyone that's what I wanted.

Nobody said anything until Rachael Edwards, who was the show-runner and also a good friend, pulled me aside. "Hey Char," she said. "You say this is how you want to do it, but you really need an audience. Can we please try it with one?"

"Nah, audiences are corny," I repeated. "I don't have any audience on *The Breakfast Club*. I don't have an audience on *The Brilliant Idiots*. Those shows work. Why can't I do it without an audience here?"

The words were coming out of my mouth, but it was really my inner child speaking. And the truth is, studio audiences make me nervous when I first get in front of them.

A lot of folks in Rachael's position would have accepted my decision, even if it was to the detriment of the show. "Hey, it's his name on the marquee, so if that's what he wants. . . ."

But Rachael kept pushing back. "Please Char, just do me a favor," she told me after we'd taped another rehearsal without an audience. "This isn't working. It feels flat."

I tried pushing back again, but Rachael dug her heels in. "Just do this," she asked. "Let's tape one time with an audience, and if you don't like it, I'll let it go. But I think you'll see it's the right move."

I knew Rachael only had my best interests at heart, so I told my inner child to calm down and agreed to tape with an audience. A minute into the taping, it was clear that Rachael was right. The audience was loving the show and I was feeding off their energy. Material that had felt flat before was suddenly landing the way it had been intended to.

I had been getting my ass handed to me in rehearsal, but a lot of people had been willing to let it slide. Not because they didn't like me, or didn't want the show to succeed. Hell, ultimately it was their asses on the line too.

But one of the reasons people settle into the role of "yes men" is because they're afraid of what might happen when they tell you no. They're worried that I might act like a diva and threaten their job. Or yell at them in a writers' room. None of those things were ever going to happen with me, but folks have seen that and way worse in the TV industry. So they learn to keep their opinions to themselves, to go with the flow, even when it's not in their best interest.

Sure, I gave Rachael a little pushback over the audience, but I never let my inner child build up such a high wall that she couldn't get through to me. Or even worse, that she was afraid to try.

And the result was an incredibly positive breakthrough for the show.

This is why it's so important to empower the people in your life to tell you what you need to hear. You have to create an environment where the people that you trust feel like they can be real with you.

It sounds simple, but it's not. Do you know how many marriages there are where one partner watches the other put on weight for years and years and never says a word? It's not that they're not thinking about it, or even obsessing over it, but they don't feel like they can say anything. They're afraid of the reaction they're going to get from their partner's inner child, so they stay silent. They might lose their attraction, begin to resent their partner, even begin to cheat, but they'll still bite their tongue for years and years.

I read a story recently about a situation like this with Busta Rhymes. Now, Busta and I have had our differences back in the day, but I really respect how he's dedicated himself to getting in shape. Busta's down a hundred pounds from where he was a few years ago, and he said the catalyst for that was a conversation he had with his then wife. In a cover story for *Men's Health*, Busta recalled how after the two had been intimate, he started having trouble breathing and felt like he was having an asthma attack. Busta says his wife was scared, but then looked at him and said, "Yo, this is not who I fell in love with."

"She didn't know what had happened outside, but she was looking at my body and the weight," Busta recalls. "She was like, 'You gotta lose this weight. This breathing is scaring me. When I met you, you wasn't like a musclehead, but you was slim, you was cut, you had your shit right. I need you to get back to who I fell in love with.'"

Busta took those words to heart and got himself right. But do you know how many men spend years and years feeling resentful over the weight their wives have put on? Just like the women who are secretly disgusted by the slobs their husbands have become, but don't ever say anything?

Thank God my wife tells me when I'm fat. Just like I thank God I feel free to give my wife a little constructive criticism when needed (though she's generally got herself together much more than I do).

No matter how old you get, or how much success you achieve in life, your inner child is still going to be sensitive and react when it hears something that makes it feel underappreciated or anxious.

That's fine. Whenever you feel that childlike voice taking over your thoughts, just breathe. Let it have its say and acknowledge what you've heard. You don't want to ignore that voice. But you can't let it dominate your thoughts either.

Have confidence that you have grown, that you have put in the work over the years to learn how to navigate situations that would have tripped you up as a child. That child's voice is trying to protect you, but don't keep those walls built up around you.

You need to create space that's going to leave room for big talk in your life. The talk you need to hear loud and clear.

Let's discuss. . . .

CHAPTER **28**

True Intentions

One of the best ways to avoid making small talk on any level is to focus on your IG. No, not your Instagram (we've already established one of the main reasons you make small talk in the first place is because of social media).

The IG I'm discussing stands for "intention" and "goals."

Let me break it down.

Every time you open your mouth or—more commonly these days—adjust your thumbs to leave a caption or comment, you have to ask yourself: "What is my intention, and what is my goal?"

Dr. Wayne W. Dyer, the author of the book *The Power of Intention*, suggests this power means giving deliberate thought today to the future you want tomorrow. So, if what you aspire to be is the number one trending topic on the World Wide Nigga Net, well, good luck.

I hate to break it to you, it's going to be hard dethroning Chrisean Rock and Blueface. But if that's what you want . . .

Now, if what you want is health (mental, emotional, physical, and spiritual), harmony in your personal relationships, creative fulfillment, real wealth, and most of all, love—then you must use the power of intention to achieve it.

I know this sounds like magical thinking, but it's true. Changing your life begins with changing your thoughts.

And you can't change your life in a meaningful way if your intentions and goals are simply to make noise.

I once heard someone in the tech world say that most people spend their lives essentially doing nothing. The big trick to social media, whether it was Twitter or Facebook, was giving people who had nothing to do, somewhere to go. Reward them with likes and follower counts so they would ignore the emptiness that was building up inside of them; social media would capture their minds and attention forever.

There's data to support this theory. A 2022 Duolingo poll revealed that the average adult wastes twenty-six days per year "doing nothing." That's 12 hours a week and more than 624 hours a year! A whopping 21 percent of that time was spent browsing social media. These social media CEOs have found a way to monetize and reward small talk!!!

According to the poll, the average adult finds themselves with absolutely nothing to do three times per day. Rather than fill that time with something meaningful, 38 percent of the respondents said that, when they had free time, they spent it watching television or looking at the internet.

I mean, you don't even need a scientific study to tell you this. Just stop next time you find yourself mindlessly scrolling through your social media feeds, trying to find something interesting to look at. Here's the reality: there's nothing there!

This is why the power of intention is important. You need real goals.

In 1999, I set my mind to working at a local radio station in Charleston, South Carolina, called Z93 Jamz.

But I wasn't content to simply work there. So, I studied the radio greats, everyone from Angie Martinez to Don Imus.

I told myself that I wanted to be on their level. I didn't want to just be a radio jock; I wanted to be a super jock.

And sure, I gravitated to a lot of "shock jocks," the kind of people who, at the time, really made historic waves in our business. I'm talking about Petey Greene, Wendy Williams, Howard Stern, Opie & Anthony, even Rush Limbaugh.

I also admired people who used their platform for public good and created real-world change. People who didn't just get on the air and start talking shit. Like Tom Joyner.

Since 1998, Tom Joyner's Tom Joyner Foundation has raised over $65 million and provided scholarships for over twenty-nine thousand students. To do something like that requires setting real intentions and real goals.

I think this is the reason why so many people do, in fact, spend their time making small talk. They lack true intentions. They lack purpose.

Because when you have a true intention—that is, some North Star that you are moving toward—you don't have time to waste doing nothing. Every minute of your life is spent trying to reach that goal.

But, if your true intention is COE (content over everything), then trust me, you do not have a true intention. You just have a mission to find even more time to waste.

And if your goal is to just simply go viral, to say whatever and do whatever just for engagement, you have lost already.

Take some of those jocks I mentioned earlier—Stern, Wendy, Limbaugh. You can easily write them off as jocks who just did stunts and talked in a way that catered to the lowest common denominator.

Even if that's all they did (which isn't something I'd agree with), what made them who they were was their commitment to the bit. They did what they did for the sake of entertainment, and even if their truth wasn't exactly the truth, what made it work was that when they got on the air every day, it sounded like they believed it.

They weren't just talking crazy; those motherfuckers *were* crazy. Or at least they made you think they were.

So, yeah, they were "shock jocks." I guess you could call them that. But at the same time, there was something substantive to what they had to offer.

Having substance makes you a wave; not having substance makes you a surfer. In fact, think about the radio jocks I just mentioned. They are all household names. Meanwhile, there are dozens of shock jocks who nobody remembers. The ones who had no substance, the ones who remained committed to shock, eventually wiped out. That's why we have to start focusing on the majors and not the minors.

That's why I wrote this book. I want to give us something BIG-GER to talk about.

There is a quote I love, from the author Morgan Richard Olivier, that has inspired me throughout this writing process:

"Teach me something. Tell me about your life experiences and the lessons you've learned. Discuss psychology and your spiritual journey. Give me depth and authenticity."

All of those things come with growth, but you have to allow yourself to grow. That's how you unlock new levels and get closer to the best version of yourself, but it starts with learning about who you are and what you are trying to accomplish. The key is larger conversations, internally and with the people around you. It will not come through small talk with others and damn sure not by making small talk with yourself. I didn't write this book for the surfers who fill mental and physical space with distractions and wait for the oceans to come and show them the way. I wrote it for the waves.

Let's discuss. . . .

CHAPTER 29

The Blessed Don't Beef
with the Miserable

Nothing will challenge your ego more than letting that small talk go from your day-to-day conversations.

Because even though small talk is what's killing us, it's becoming harder and harder to avoid. Nowadays everyone and their mother is trying to speak for a living. Everyone is a social media influencer. And there's not a day that goes by where they don't feel like they have to share their thoughts with the world.

The result is that we're being besieged by a never-ending cascade of thoughts, opinions, rants, lectures, and "reads."

Back in the day, you weren't actually subjected to hearing that many people's opinions. At least not through the media. There were three national news channels to choose between and a handful of local channels. There was an old white guy named Andy Rooney on *60 Minutes* who had the "rant" game on lock. Each week he'd end the show by ranting about something like how it's hard to tell the difference between diet and regular soda, how mixed nuts weren't mixed evenly. Today he'd barely get reposted, but back in the eighties and nineties people ate it up.

Then in the newspapers (remember those?) there would be syndicated columnists who would share their opinions. They might share their weekly take on politics or cultural movements.

But other than that, you pretty much got exposed to other people's opinions by talking to them in person. You might meet them at a party, on the street, or at a friend's house. And if they started going in on a subject, you'd be able to size them up then and there. Remember, there's no cuts and edits live. There's no adjusting the lighting live. Just words and energy in real time. And you'd be able to decide pretty quickly, "Yeah, I don't need to pay this fool any mind." Or you might think, "You know what, this guy is making some sense. Let me keep listening." Or even better, you might disagree with something being said and get into an actual debate. Where you go back and forth on an issue or an idea, not to see how many likes you can get, but because you're both truly passionate about the idea.

Those days are long, long gone.

Instead, you're subjected to everyone's ideas, all at once. Experts and idiots, fools and philosophers, are all broadcast at the same volume. Remember in school they had kids separated into honors classes, regular classes, and "slow classes"? Well the problem with social media is they got all of us on it together and we not supposed to be. On social media, everyone's lumped together and it's impossible to tell who is who.

I used to joke that segregation was a great idea, it was just poorly executed. It should have been based on behavior not race. And social media is really reinforcing that belief. If we really segregated social media and separated the fools and loudmouths from those who are knowledgeable and have something meaningful to say, man it would be such a more rewarding experience!

But because there is no social media segregation, you have to learn how to keep yourself away from fools and blowhards on your own. If you come across a post that is filled with lies, half-truths, misinformation, and a poorly presented perspective, please just keep moving! You don't have to stop and type out a reply. After all, have you ever truly felt better after replying to a stupid post? I highly doubt it.

Besides, replying to something is what these platforms want you to do. The more you argue with people who disagree with you, the more time you're engaged. And that's what the folks at TikTok, IG, X, Facebook, and YouTube all want. You could spend hours, days, even weeks going back and forth with people over an opinion. And chances are that it's about a subject that is extremely small in the grand scheme of things.

Successful people don't waste their time arguing online. If they put an opinion out there, they don't spend a lot of time worrying about who agrees with it or not. They understand that there are billions of people in this world with almost as many opinions, so some folks will agree, some folks will disagree, and some people simply won't care. All of those reactions are perfectly fine.

They also understand that most of the people who take issue with you actually don't have anything against you, they are just trying to get their "business" going. They are doing this for whatever audience they have grown to have on social media and you are just their content for today.

Whenever I see someone go on an impassioned rant against another person, I'm always skeptical of their true agenda. When I see folks using language like "I hate this person," or "This person is the scum of the earth," I can't take them seriously. They're speaking with authority on people they don't even know. It makes me wonder what trauma they're dealing with in their own lives that they feel the need to project onto others.

There's a basic formula I try to remember, which is, "Happy people don't hate and hating people aren't happy."

So please, when someone is attacking you or trying to take you down in the public sphere, don't fall into their trap. Remember, they're not fighting you, they're fighting their own demons.

They're not trying to change your mind, or even make you see things their way. All they want you to do is respond. That's it. Again, their real goal is engagement. Because in this sick, twisted world we currently live in, your response somehow validates whatever they said. You replied to them, so y'all must be on the same level. They must be a peer of some sort.

But again, think about who you're really engaging with in these circumstances. It's not college professors or philosophers or journalists sitting in an office lined with books who've come to their opinions after years of research. The person you're arguing with is probably literally sitting on the toilet with their pants down around their ankles, Pornhub on the laptop, and . . . let me stop there.

Or they're forty-plus years old, on a broken-down desktop in their mother's basement. Or they're sitting on a folding chair bored out of their minds during their overnight security guard shift at Walmart. Their faces are filled with acne. They haven't seen their penis in years because their guts are spilling over their waistline. Half of them aren't old enough to vote and the other half have yet to make their mothers proud in any way, shape, or form. These miserable people are the ones you want to argue with? And let's not even get into the Bot game, you got your blood pressure up beefing with A.I. on social media??

Because trust, that is who you're talking to when you engage in these conversations.

This is some of the worst small talk to partake in because what these people feel about you is so small in the grand scheme of things. Don't engage with these miserable people under any circumstances! Not small talk, big talk, honest talk, real talk—no conversation is to be had with these folks because there is simply no win. Can I speak to my trauma survivors for one quick second? Dr. Glenn Patrick Doyle once said, "Trauma survivors often develop SEVERE aversion to 'small talk.' Sometimes superficial chitchat even makes us annoyed or angry. It's nothing personal—we've just gotten REAL clear on how precious our bandwidth is and REAL selective on how we're willing to allocate it."

It's simple: we don't have time for the fuck shit, we've come too far, survived too much, did too much inner work to be dealing with the small talk that this world will serve us for FREE.99 every day.

That's why I want to end this conversation with you by stressing that although you're up against some formidable forces—social media, apathy, envy, entitlement, and untreated trauma (*which you need to go treat ASAP*)—there are still so many ways you can improve how you communicate with the world!

Just because everybody else is communicating through their phones on the most surface level possible doesn't mean it's OK. It doesn't mean it's healthy.

Remember, there was a time in this country where it seemed like everyone was smoking a pack of cigarettes a day. Didn't mean that it was healthy! Folks just didn't understand how deadly those cancer sticks were yet.

We're in a similar stage right now in terms of how we communicate (or don't) with each other. Just because everyone else is engaging in small talk their entire lives doesn't mean they're not going to pay a price for it down the road.

As soon as you put this book down for the final time, please take some of the concepts I've discussed and share them with the world. Participate in a meaningful conversation you've been putting off. Address a trauma that you've been running from your whole life. Refuse to get drawn into what your algorithm is telling you and do your own research. Come to your own conclusion.

Get honest or die lying. You don't want your tombstone to read "Here Lies a Liar," do you? So take this opportunity right now to not just be honest with yourself, but with everyone around you too. The life you save by doing that will more than likely be your own.

Let's discuss. . . .

Acknowledgments

I want to start by acknowledging my mother for keeping me in the Kingdom Hall as a child. It inspired me more than she probably realizes. If you were like me and grew up as a Jehovah's Witness back in the 1900s, then you will never forget *My Book of Bible Stories* with its gold cover and red lettering. Now take a look at the cover of this book again. You see what I did there? Thank you, Mom.

I also want to thank the incredible team over at Simon & Schuster and Black Privilege Publishing: Jonathan Karp, Libby McGuire, Nicholas Ciani, Shida Carr, and Hannah Frankel. And as always, thanks to Jan Miller and Ali Kominsky from Dupree Miller and Chris Morrow for helping bring this book to life.

Coming from South Carolina, where the first anti-literacy laws for slaves were created back in 1739, the significance of having an actual publishing company is not lost on me. As a descendant of those brave enslaved people who were denied so much, including the right to read, knowing I'm blessed with the ability to reach the world through the power of words means everything to me.